BECOME MORE THAN A CONQUEROR

ATHLETIC
FAITH

GREATER IS HE
YES AND AMEN
BE BOLD
ONLY BELIEVE
REJOICE IN TRIALS
DO IT NOW

BY CHRISTIAN SANLEGO

Scripture Quotations

Publishing Information

Published in Australia by **Self-Published**
eBook ISBN: 978-1-7640566-1-8
EPUB ISBN: 978-1-7640566-1-8
Print ISBN: 978-1-7640566-0-1
Audiobook ISBN: 978-1-7640566-2-5

For permissions, inquiries, or bulk orders, contact: books@sanlego.com

Disclaimer

This book is a work of faith-based inspiration. The author and publisher

Dedication of Rights

By the grace of God, this work is dedicated to the encouragement and strengthening of believers in their walk of faith. May it bring glory to Jesus Christ and bless those who read it.

Contents

Preface   1

1. The Starting Line   5

2. The Coach   10

3. The Playbook   19

4. The Training Ground   26

5. The Teammate   35

6. Are you ready to train?   43

7. Fitness Test   55

8. Joy   58

9. Peace I   68

10. Peace II   76

11. Rest in the Race   82

12. Patience   90

13. Kindness   98

14. Goodness   105

15. Faithfulness   115

16. Gentleness   122

17. Self-Control   129

18. Love   139

19. Elite's Training   153

Recognizing the Enemy's Traps   158

20. Fear   160

21. Pride   167

22. Anger   172

23. Distraction   178

24. Building Spiritual Endurance   183

25. The Power of Correction   189

26. Finishing Strong   196

27. Your End... His New Begining in You   201

Preface

This book is the fruit of a revelation the Holy Spirit placed in my heart—a modern-day analogy for those who have been athletes or have experienced the effort, discipline, and perseverance of competitive sports. Whether you are just starting your journey of faith or seeking to grow stronger in it, my prayer is that this book will encourage you, challenge you, and equip you to build a faith that endures.

Through this revelation, I came to understand that **faith is not the same for everyone**. We are all equally loved by our amazing God, without distinction—but our levels of faith and the strength we build in it **impact how prepared we are to withstand the storms, trials, and tribulations of life**.

We see this truth reflected in Scripture:

- There is the faith of **Thomas**, who needed to

see before he could believe.

- There is the faith of the **Centurion**, who understood that true power and authority required only a word to be spoken.

In our case, that word is the Word of God—the Bible. And the living Word is Jesus Himself. If we believe Him when He says, *"Do not worry,"* and when He declares, *"You are more than a conqueror,"* then that foundation is what allows us to build our faith *as an athlete builds strength, endurance, and skill.*

This book is an analogy for us to grasp this truth: **building a strong faith, and sustaining it through life, requires discipline—just like an athlete preparing for a match, a race, or a fierce opponent.** It requires training, perseverance, and a deep reliance on the guidance of our ultimate coach, the Holy Spirit.

But let me be clear—**our efforts do not earn us salvation.** That is a gift, freely given through Jesus Christ. However, **training our faith like an athlete allows us to endure the race, overcome challenges, and—best of all—be equipped to help others when**

they face their own storms.

So, as you read these pages, may you be strengthened, encouraged, and reminded that faith is a journey. And just like any athlete who commits to training, growth, and perseverance, you, too, can build a faith that stands firm, finishes the race, and helps others do the same.

Let's train together. Let's grow together. Let's run this race of faith to the very end.

Christian SanLego

Chapter 1

The Starting Line

The Foundation of Faith

E very race has a starting line, and for the Athlete of Faith, the starting line is marked by one word: *grace.* Grace is where everything begins. It's the unearned, undeserved gift of salvation that God offers to each of us through Jesus Christ. Without it, we couldn't even step onto the track.

Ephesians 2:8-9 reminds us:

> *"God saved you by his grace when you believed. And you can't take credit for this; it is a gift from God. Salvation is not a reward for the good things we have done, so none of us can boast about it."*

Grace isn't something we achieve—it's something we receive. It's God's way of saying, "You don't have to be perfect. I've already made a way for you." Yet so many of us struggle to truly embrace grace. We either try to earn it through good works or reject it, feeling unworthy. But grace isn't about who we are; it's about who God is.

Letting Go of Shame

Before we can move forward in our journey of faith, we need to leave behind the baggage of shame. Shame whispers lies: "You're not good enough. You'll never measure up. Look at all the mistakes you've made." But Jesus came to silence those lies.

Romans 8:1 declares:

> *"So now there is no condemnation for those who belong to Christ Jesus."*

If you've accepted Jesus as your Savior, your past mistakes no longer define you. They're covered by His blood, and you've been made new.

Here's a practical exercise to help let go of shame:

Write It Down: Take a moment to write down anything you're ashamed of—mistakes, regrets, or failures.

Lay It at His Feet: Pray over the list, asking Jesus to take your shame and replace it with His peace.

Tear It Up: Physically destroy the list as a symbol of God's forgiveness and your fresh start.

Understanding Grace as a Transformative Power

Grace doesn't just save us—it transforms us. It's the fuel that empowers us to live differently, to break free from the chains of sin, and to grow into the people God created us to be.

Titus 2:11-12 explains:

> *"For the grace of God has been revealed, bringing salvation to all people. And we are instructed to turn from godless living and sinful pleasures. We should live in this evil world with wisdom, righteousness, and devotion to God."*

Think of grace like a seed planted in your heart. For it to grow, it needs care—prayer, scripture, and a willingness to trust God. The more you lean into His grace, the more it changes you from the inside out.

Reflection Prompt

- What does grace mean to you personally?

- Are there areas of your life where you struggle to accept God's grace?

- How would your life look different if you fully embraced the freedom that grace offers?

Practical Exercises

Memorize a Verse About Grace: Choose a verse that resonates with you (e.g., Ephesians 2:8-9) and meditate on it throughout the week.

Practice Grace Toward Others: Identify one way you can show grace to someone in your life. It could be forgiving a wrong, offering encouragement, or being patient in a challenging situation.

Start a Grace Journal: Each day, write down one way

you've experienced God's grace. It might be a kind word from a friend, an answered prayer, or simply the beauty of a sunrise.

Closing Prayer

Lord, thank You for the gift of grace. Help me to fully accept it, to let go of shame, and to walk in the freedom You've given me. Teach me to rely on Your strength and to reflect Your love to those around me. In Jesus' name, **Amen.**

Chapter 2

The Coach

The Holy Spirit

No great athlete trains alone. Behind every champion is a coach—someone who sees their potential, guides their training, corrects their mistakes, and prepares them to endure the toughest challenges. Even the most talented athlete can lose direction, make avoidable mistakes, or burn out without proper guidance.

In our journey of faith, the **Holy Spirit is our Coach**—our personal Trainer who equips us to overcome trials, resist the traps of the enemy, and develop the endurance needed to live a Spirit-led life that reflects Jesus' love.

"And I will ask the Father, and he will give you another Advocate, who will never leave you.

He is the Holy Spirit, who leads into all truth."
— John 14:16-17

Training for a Different Kind of Victory

This chapter is not about *winning* the Christian race in the way the world defines victory. It's about:

Overcoming the enemy's traps.

Enduring hardship without being shaken.

Living a life led by the Spirit—a life that reflects Jesus in all areas.

God doesn't just want us to survive—He wants us to **thrive**, to experience His abundant life here on earth, just as it is in heaven.

The Holy Spirit—Our Personal Trainer

In **1 Corinthians 9:24-27**, Paul compares the Christian life to a race and a boxing match. He emphasizes discipline, focus, and perseverance—not because we are trying to *earn* something, but because without training, we will fall into the enemy's traps.

*"So I do not run aimlessly, nor do I box
as though beating the air; but I discipline
my body and keep it under control, lest
after preaching to others I myself should be
disqualified." —* 1 Corinthians 9:26-27

Paul is saying: **This race is real. This fight is real.**
We are not just shadowboxing—we are engaged in a
spiritual battle (*Ephesians 6:12*). The Holy Spirit is the
one who prepares us, giving us the right **drills and
challenges** so we are not caught off guard when trials
come.

Drills and Challenges: Training Through Trials

An athlete doesn't only train in good weather.
They train in the cold, in the rain, even when
exhausted—because they know the race won't be
easy. Likewise, the Holy Spirit allows us to face
challenges, **not to break us, but to train us.**

*"Consider it pure joy, my brothers and sisters,
whenever you face trials of many kinds,*

because you know that the testing of your
faith produces perseverance." — James 1:2-3

Every challenge is a **training session** designed to prepare us:

Difficult people train us in patience and kindness.

Seasons of lack train us in trust and contentment.

Moments of failure train us in grace and humility.

God is **not punishing us**—He is **coaching us, strengthening us** so that we can withstand storms and help others when they face their own.

Conditioning Against the Enemy's Attacks

In boxing, an untrained fighter is vulnerable—not because they lack strength, but because they don't know how to defend themselves. The enemy knows that if he can't make us fall, he will try to make us *feel* defeated.

Common Traps of the Enemy

Shame: "You messed up again. God is disappointed in you."

Distraction: "Focus on your problems, not on God's promises."

Comparison: "Look how strong others are—you're not good enough."

The Holy Spirit teaches us how to counter these traps:

Against **shame** → He reminds us that we are covered by grace (*Romans 8:1*).

Against **distraction** → He shifts our focus back to God's truth (*John 16:13*).

Against **comparison** → He reminds us of our unique purpose (*Ephesians 2:10*).

Just like an athlete learns how to dodge blows and keep their stance, **we must let the Holy Spirit train us to stand firm against these attacks.**

Strength Training—The Fruits of the Spirit

A champion is not only skilled but also **disciplined**. They don't just avoid mistakes—they build **strength**. In the Christian life, our **strength** comes from the

Fruits of the Spirit:

> *"But the fruit of the Spirit is love, joy, peace, patience, kindness, goodness, faithfulness, gentleness, and self-control."* — Galatians 5:22-23

These qualities equip us to:

Endure hardship without losing faith.

Respond to attacks with grace instead of anger.

Encourage and restore others with gentleness.

We don't develop these fruits overnight—they grow through **training.**

We build **patience** when tested by difficult situations.

We build **kindness** by choosing it even when it's hard.

We build **faith** by trusting God in seasons of uncertainty.

The Holy Spirit **doesn't just give us** these qualities—He **develops them in us.**

Equipped to Serve Others

The goal of training is not just personal growth—it is also to **equip us to help others.**

> *"Brothers and sisters, if someone is caught in a sin, you who live by the Spirit should restore that person gently."* — Galatians 6:1

If we are led by emotions instead of the Spirit, we will react:

In **pride** instead of humility.

In **frustration** instead of patience.

In **self-righteousness** instead of love.

But when we allow the Holy Spirit to train us, **we gain the endurance, wisdom, and gentleness to lift others up rather than tear them down.**

> *"For even the Son of Man did not come to be served, but to serve, and to give his life as a ransom for many."* — Mark 10:45

Final Reflection: Train, Endure, Serve

The Holy Spirit is here to **train us**—to equip us to withstand trials, overcome the traps of the enemy, and live a life that reflects Jesus' abundant life.

We are not just running for ourselves—we are training to **become a source of strength for others.**

Let's allow the Holy Spirit to train us.

Let's embrace challenges as part of the process.

And when we stand firm, let's use our strength to lift others.

Because a life led by the Spirit is **a life that changes lives.**

Ways the Holy Spirit Speaks to Us:

Through Scripture: The Spirit brings God's Word to life, applying it to our situations.

In Prayer: As we pray, the Spirit guides our thoughts and stirs our hearts.

Through Peace: The Spirit often confirms decisions with a deep sense of peace.

In Conviction: The Spirit gently corrects us when we're heading in the wrong direction.

Practical Exercises to Strengthen Your Connection:

Daily Prayer Time: Set aside 10 minutes each day to ask the Holy Spirit for guidance and listen quietly.

Scripture Meditation: Choose a passage and ask the Spirit to reveal its meaning in your life.

Journaling: Write down moments when you sense the Spirit's guidance.

Closing Prayer

Holy Spirit, thank You for being my Trainer and Advocate. Help me to recognize Your voice and follow Your lead. Empower me to live boldly for Jesus, and equip me to fulfill the purpose You've given me. Teach me to trust You in every area of my life. In Jesus' name, ***Amen.***

Chapter 3

The Playbook

The Word of God

E very great athlete understands that success isn't accidental—it's the result of careful preparation, discipline, and strategy. Imagine a mountaineer attempting to scale a dangerous peak without studying the terrain, understanding the weather conditions, or packing the right equipment. Without a guide, a map, and the necessary training, they are not only unprepared but also at serious risk. One wrong move, one unexpected storm, and their journey could end in failure—or worse, disaster.

Now, think of a boxer stepping into the ring without studying their opponent or refining their technique. They might have raw strength, but without footwork, defensive skills, and a strategy to anticipate attacks, they will be quickly overwhelmed. A champion doesn't rely on talent alone—they train relentlessly, reviewing past fights, learning from mistakes, and adjusting their approach based on what works.

Athletes don't just rely on their own experience; they learn from others who have gone before them. **They study past victories and defeats, incorporate new techniques, and adapt to changing circumstances.**

In the same way, as **athletes of faith**, we need a **playbook**—a **source of wisdom, guidance, and strategy** that helps us navigate life's challenges. **The Bible is that playbook.** It is more than just a collection of ancient stories—it is a divinely inspired training manual filled with instructions, warnings, and examples that help us grow stronger in faith.

The stories in Scripture are not random events; they were written **for our benefit**. **We learn from the victories and mistakes of those who have walked before us.** We see the consequences of disobedience and the rewards of faithfulness. Just as athletes study the best techniques and training methods of past champions, we must **study God's Word to strengthen our spiritual endurance and overcome life's battles.**

But it's not just about **knowing** what God has given us. A mountaineer may have the best gear, but if they don't know how to use it, they are still unprepared. A boxer may have great advice from their coach, but if they don't apply it in the ring, they will still lose the fight.

Likewise, it is not enough to simply **know** that Jesus has given us power and authority through His sacrifice on the cross. **That power is only activated when we live in alignment with God's Word**—when it shapes our thoughts, decisions, and actions. The strength of our faith is directly connected to our preparation in Scripture.

Jesus **is the Word** (John 1:1), and when we train in Scripture, we **tune our hearts to His voice.** The more we immerse ourselves in God's truth, the more we recognize His direction and align ourselves with His love and authority.

That's why, when storms come our way, we can stand firm and declare, **"Peace, be still"** (Mark 4:39). **Because we are not just repeating words—we are speaking from a place of alignment with God's truth, power, and love.**

A well-trained athlete doesn't crumble under pressure—they rise to the challenge. And when we are trained in the Word, we won't be shaken by trials, temptations, or attacks. Instead, we will stand firm, walk in confidence, and help others do the same.

Biblical Insight: Our Source of Strength

Paul, a spiritual coach to many, emphasized the importance of God's Word to Timothy:

> *"All Scripture is God-breathed and is useful for teaching, rebuking, correcting and training in righteousness, so that the servant of God may be thoroughly equipped for every good work."* — 2 Timothy 3:16-17

Just as a coach corrects mistakes and refines techniques, **Scripture teaches us what is right, convicts us when we stray, and strengthens us to grow in faith.**

Athletes don't guess their way through training. They follow strict routines, reviewing playbooks and refining their form. Likewise, we must **approach**

Scripture with discipline and consistency, studying it daily to build **spiritual endurance**.

Even Jesus demonstrated this. When He was tempted in the wilderness, He didn't rely on emotions or personal strength. Instead, He responded with Scripture:

"It is written..." — Matthew 4:4,7,10

The Word was **His weapon**, and it is **ours too**.

Practical Wisdom: Training in the Word

A dedicated athlete doesn't train only when they feel like it. They wake up early, push through fatigue, and practice even when it's difficult. In the same way, **we must develop a habit of daily Bible study.** Here's how:

Read with Purpose – Approach Scripture as a personal message from God. Ask, *What is God teaching me today?*

Meditate and Memorize – Just as athletes rehearse plays until they become second nature, we must store

God's Word in our hearts (**Psalm 119:11**).

Apply What You Learn – Faith without action is like training without competing. Live out what Scripture teaches (**James 1:22**).

Pray Through Scripture – Use God's Word in your prayers, declaring His promises over your life.

Stay Consistent – A one-time workout won't make an athlete strong. Make daily Scripture reading a **non-negotiable** part of your routine.

When we train in the Word, we become **equipped to face challenges, endure trials, and help others** who are struggling in their own races.

Reflection Prompts

- How often do I intentionally spend time in God's Word?

- Do I see the Bible as a training manual, or do I treat it casually?

- What scriptures have helped me in times of struggle?

- How can I make Scripture a greater part of my daily life?

Closing Prayer

Heavenly Father,
Thank You for giving us Your Word as our training manual. Help me to love Scripture, study it with passion, and apply it with wisdom. I desire to be equipped, strong, and prepared for every challenge in my race of faith.

Teach me to run with perseverance and live by Your truth. Holy Spirit, guide me in understanding and remind me of Scripture in moments of need. May my life be shaped by Your Word so that I can be a light to others.

*In Jesus' name, **Amen.***

Chapter 4

The Training Ground

The Church

Imagine an elite athlete trying to train alone—no coach to refine their technique, no teammates to challenge them, no support system to help them recover from injuries. They may have raw talent, but without the right environment, their growth is limited.

Faith works the same way. God never intended for us to walk this journey alone. While the Holy Spirit works within us, He also works **through others** to strengthen, refine, and equip us. Just as elite athletes need structured training environments to reach peak performance, **we need the Church—the ultimate training ground for spiritual endurance, growth, and transformation.**

The Church isn't just a building. It's a **team** of believers, learning, healing, and growing together in Christ. It's where **new Christians** find their footing, where **mature believers** refine their spiritual disciplines, and where **leaders** are equipped to help others grow. This cycle of transformation prepares us to withstand the traps of the enemy and live Spirit-led lives.

> *"And let us not neglect our meeting together, as some people do, but encourage one another, especially now that the day of his return is drawing near." — Hebrews 10:25*

The Church: God's Spiritual Training Ground

The Book of Acts gives us a clear picture of how the early Church functioned as a **spiritual training ground:**

At **Pentecost**, the disciples were **gathered together** when the Holy Spirit filled them, empowering them to preach with boldness (**Acts 2:1-4**).

When **Peter and John were threatened**, the believers **prayed together**, and the Holy Spirit gave them courage to keep preaching (**Acts 4:23-31**).

The first Church devoted itself to **fellowship, teaching, prayer, and breaking bread**, leading to explosive spiritual and numerical growth (**Acts 2:42-47**).

God's design is clear: **we are meant to be part of something bigger than ourselves.** The Holy Spirit moves powerfully when believers are united in faith, just as a team thrives when players work together toward a shared goal.

> *"Two people are better off than one, for they can help each other succeed. If one person falls, the other can reach out and help. But someone who falls alone is in real trouble." — Ecclesiastes 4:9-10*

What Makes a Strong Training Ground?

An athlete cannot reach peak performance by training alone. They need **the right environment, guidance, and support**—just as we do in our spiritual walk.

The Right Training Facility

Elite athletes train in **specialized facilities** equipped with everything they need—coaches, strength equipment, recovery areas. A strong church provides:

Bible studies to deepen knowledge.

Prayer groups for encouragement.

Discipleship programs to refine spiritual maturity.

Community service to practice faith in action.

A **church rooted in God's Word** is like a high-performance training center—it prepares believers to thrive.

A Recovery and Healing Team

Athletes experience **injuries** and need physiotherapists, nutritionists, and mental health experts. Likewise, believers go through **spiritual wounds—doubt, fear, burnout, or sin.**

The Church provides:

Pastoral care for spiritual healing.

Encouragement from fellow believers.

Prayer and deliverance to restore strength.

The Church is **not** a place for perfect people—it's a place where **broken people come to heal.**

Stretching and Strengthening

Growth happens when we're **pushed beyond our comfort zone.** A strong church challenges us to step out in faith by:

Serving others in ministry.

Sharing our testimony.

Taking on leadership roles.

Trusting God in difficult seasons.

Like an athlete increasing resistance to grow stronger, **we grow when we allow God to stretch us.**

Expert Coaching for Every Area of Life

Athletes don't just train physically—they receive coaching in **nutrition, mental toughness, and game strategy.** The Church provides:

Spiritual Coaching – Pastors and mentors guide us in

Scripture.

Emotional Coaching – Small groups and friendships provide support.

Financial Coaching – Biblical teaching on stewardship and generosity.

Relational Coaching – Marriage and family ministries strengthen relationships.

Purpose Coaching – Guidance to integrate faith into work and daily life.

A **thriving church** develops well-rounded believers **who reflect Christ in every area of life.**

The Enemy's Strategy: Isolation

Satan knows the **power of community**, which is why **one of his greatest strategies is isolation.** He plants lies like:

"I don't need church—I can grow on my own."

"My faith is private."

"Church is full of hypocrites."

"I'm too busy to join a group or serve."

But just as an athlete who **skips training weakens over time**, a Christian who isolates themselves from the Church **becomes spiritually vulnerable.**

"Stay alert! Watch out for your great enemy, the devil. He prowls around like a roaring lion, looking for someone to devour." — 1 Peter 5:8

A lion **always** attacks the weakest, most isolated prey. This is why the Bible warns us **not** to neglect meeting together. When we stay connected, we **grow stronger** and are **better equipped** to resist the enemy's schemes.

Your Role in the Training Ground

Being part of the Church isn't just about **attending** once a week—it's about **actively engaging** in God's training ground. Here's how you can maximize your spiritual growth:

Commit to Regular Training – Engage in Bible study, prayer, and worship.

Find a Team – Join a small group or serve in a ministry.

Stay Accountable – Have mentors and fellow believers encourage you.

Stretch Yourself – Step out in faith and take on new challenges.

Help Others Grow – Discipleship isn't just about receiving; it's about **passing on what you've learned.**

When **athletes train in top facilities with strong coaches and teammates, they excel.** When **believers train in God's Church, surrounded by His people and guided by His Spirit, they thrive.**

Final Thought

The Church is **not perfect**—just like no gym is free of beginners or struggling athletes. But **it is necessary.** It is the place where **grace abounds, faith strengthens, and transformation happens.**

> *"As iron sharpens iron, so one person sharpens another." — Proverbs 27:17*

You need the Church, and the Church needs

you. Step onto the training ground. **Grow. Heal. Train. And then—help others do the same.**

Reflection Questions:

- How has being part of a church community helped you grow spiritually?

- Are there areas where you've been isolating yourself? How can you reconnect?

- What steps can you take to be more engaged in your church?

Closing Prayer

*Lord, thank You for the gift of the Church. Help me to stay connected, grow stronger, and encourage others. Guide me to use my gifts to build up the body of Christ. Keep me from isolation and strengthen me through Your people. In Jesus' name, **Amen.***

Chapter 5

The Teammate

Immanuel

"And be sure of this: I am with you always, even to the end of the age." — Matthew 28:20

We live in a world that celebrates individual achievement. "Make it on your own." "Hustle harder." "Be self-made." Everywhere we turn, the message is the same—success depends on you and you alone.

But this mindset leads to exhaustion. When we try to handle everything by ourselves, we eventually hit a wall. We weren't created to row through life alone. From the very beginning, God designed us for relationship—with Him and with others.

That's why one of the most powerful names of Jesus

is *Immanuel*—"God with us." He isn't just a distant
Savior, watching from the sidelines. He's in the boat
with you, rowing alongside you, sharing the weight,
and guiding you through every storm.

Trust Your Teammate

If you've ever watched a rowing team, you'll notice
something important: they don't just rely on their own
strength. Every rower moves in sync, trusting each
other to keep the rhythm. The moment one person
tries to do it all on their own, the whole boat loses
balance.

Now, imagine Jesus in that boat with you. But
instead of letting Him row, you keep trying to do
all the work yourself—straining, pushing, exhausting
yourself—while He patiently waits for you to hand over
some of the weight.

So many of us live this way. We believe in Jesus, but
we don't let Him be our teammate. We keep rowing
harder, thinking we have to handle everything alone.
But faith isn't about striving—it's about trusting the
One who is rowing with you.

Your Refuge and Strenght

There's a moment in the Bible when Jesus' disciples were caught in a storm. These men were experienced fishermen, but the waves overwhelmed them. They panicked, afraid they wouldn't make it. But Jesus? He was right there in the boat.

> *"Then He climbed into the boat, and the wind stopped. They were totally amazed." —* Mark 6:51

Jesus didn't stand on the shore shouting instructions. He *got in the boat*. He was present in the storm, just as He is present in every storm you face.

> *"God is our refuge and strength, always ready to help in times of trouble." —* Psalm 46:1

Maybe you're going through something difficult right now—stress, failure, loneliness, uncertainty. Maybe you feel like you're rowing against the wind, making no progress. The good news? You don't have to fight it alone. Jesus is right there. All you have to do is let Him row with you.

Led by the Spirit

Every great rowing team has a coxswain—the person who sits at the back of the boat, steering, setting the pace, and calling out instructions. The rowers provide the power, but the coxswain gives direction, ensuring they move efficiently and in perfect rhythm.

In your faith journey, the Holy Spirit is your coxswain. He is the One who keeps you on course, guiding you toward God's purpose. Without Him, you might row in the wrong direction, waste your energy, or even capsize in the storms of life.

> *"When the Spirit of truth comes, He will guide you into all truth. He will not speak on His own but will tell you what He has heard. He will tell you about the future."*— John 16:13

Many believers struggle because they try to row without listening to the coxswain. They move in their own strength, ignore God's direction, and wonder why they feel lost or exhausted. But when you tune in to the

Holy Spirit, He keeps you in sync with Jesus, directing your strokes and ensuring you stay on course.

The Holy Spirit doesn't just give commands—He encourages. A great coxswain calls out to the rowers, pushing them forward when they're tired, reminding them of the goal, and making sure they don't lose heart. That's exactly what the Holy Spirit does for us.

> *"Your own ears will hear Him. Right behind you a voice will say, 'This is the way you should go,' whether to the right or to the left."*
> — Isaiah 30:21

When you feel weak, the Holy Spirit reminds you of God's strength.

When you're uncertain, He gives you wisdom.

When you drift off course, He gently corrects you and brings you back.

A rowing team that ignores the coxswain will never win the race. A believer who ignores the Holy Spirit will struggle unnecessarily. But when you learn to listen, trust, and follow His guidance, your faith journey becomes steady, powerful, and full of peace.

Team Spirit

In a rowing team, the key to winning isn't individual strength—it's synchronization. If each rower moves at a different pace, the boat slows down or even drifts off course. But when they follow the lead of their coxswain and trust their teammates, the boat glides forward with power and efficiency.

Jesus is your teammate, rowing beside you. The Holy Spirit is your coxswain, guiding the rhythm and direction. Your role? Stay in sync with them.

"So I say, let the Holy Spirit guide your lives. Then you won't be doing what your sinful nature craves. The sinful nature wants to do evil, which is just the opposite of what the Spirit wants. And the Spirit gives us desires that are the opposite of what the sinful nature desires. These two forces are constantly fighting each other, so you are not free to carry out your good intentions." — Galatians 5:16-17

Jesus doesn't just help you row; He teaches you how to move with Him—how to work from a place of peace, not panic. The Holy Spirit sets the rhythm, ensuring that you stay in step with God's plan.

Reflection Prompts

- Are there areas in your life where you've been rowing alone?

- What would it look like to fully trust Jesus as your teammate?

- Are you moving in sync with Jesus, or are you trying to row at your own pace?

- Do you listen to the Holy Spirit, or do you find yourself ignoring His guidance?

Action Steps

Invite Jesus into Your Boat – Surrender your struggles to Him in prayer.

Row in Sync with Christ – Follow His lead instead of relying on your own strength.

Listen to the Holy Spirit – Ask Him for wisdom, guidance, and encouragement.

Trust His Timing – When life feels uncertain, remember that Jesus is always present, and the Holy Spirit is directing your course.

Closing Prayer

Thank You Jesus for being my Immanuel—God with me. I confess that too often, I try to row through life on my own, relying on my own strength instead of trusting in You. Help me to surrender, to move in sync with You, and to let You take the weight I was never meant to carry alone. Holy Spirit, I invite You to be my coxswain—directing my course, setting the pace, and leading me in truth. Teach me to listen, to trust, and to row in rhythm with Your will. Thank You for being in the boat with me.
In Jesus' name, **Amen.**

Chapter 6

Are you ready to train?

F ormula 1 drivers are some of the most highly trained athletes in the world. Their reflexes are razor-sharp, their endurance allows them to withstand the intense physical and mental demands of a race, and their ability to read the track and anticipate challenges is second to none. Every race is different—different weather conditions, different track layouts, different opponents—but through years of training, these drivers learn to navigate every twist and turn with precision and confidence.

The race of faith is no different. The Bible tells us that our journey is not a leisurely Sunday drive but a race that requires endurance, focus, and discipline (Hebrews 12:1-2). Unlike a Formula 1 driver, however, we don't race for a temporary trophy. We race with an eternal purpose—to grow in our relationship with

Jesus, to reflect His character, and to bring His love to those around us.

But before we go any further, let's be clear: this training is not what *saves* us. Salvation is a free gift of grace, as we established in the first chapter. We don't earn our place in God's family through effort, just as a Formula 1 driver doesn't earn the ability to drive simply by practicing. The ability to drive comes first, then training refines and develops that ability. In the same way, once we are saved, the Holy Spirit begins His work in us, shaping us into Christ's likeness.

God has given us both a **training program** (the Bible) and a **Coach** (the Holy Spirit) to guide us. Why? Because, whether we like it or not, this race is full of opposition. The devil's mission is to steal, kill, and destroy (John 10:10), and he will use every curve, detour, and distraction to take us off course. But Jesus has already overcome the world (John 16:33), and He has given us His Spirit—the same power that raised Jesus from the dead—to help us train, build endurance, and navigate life's toughest tracks.

But here's the big question: **How do we know if we're on the right track?**

The Diagnostic System of Faith

In an F1 car, sensors provide a continuous stream of data to ensure optimal performance. There are sensors for tire pressure, fuel levels, engine temperature, and even blind-spot detection. These sensors allow the driver and the pit crew to diagnose problems early, make necessary adjustments, and prevent major failures.

But what about you and me? How do we know if we are driving our faith in the right direction? How do we diagnose whether we are following the Holy Spirit's guidance or drifting off track?

The Bible gives us a **spiritual sensor system**, found in **2 Peter 1:2-8**:

> *2 May God give you more and more grace and peace as you grow in your knowledge of God and Jesus our Lord.*
>
> ***Growing in Faith***
> *3 By his divine power, God has given us everything we need for living a godly life.*

*We have received all of this by coming
to know him, the one who called us to
himself by means of his marvelous glory
and excellence. 4 And because of his glory
and excellence, he has given us great and
precious promises. These are the promises
that enable you to share his divine nature
and escape the world's corruption caused by
human desires.*

*5 In view of all this, make every effort
to respond to God's promises. Supplement
your faith with a generous provision of
moral excellence, and moral excellence
with knowledge, 6 and knowledge with
self-control, and self-control with patient
endurance, and patient endurance with
godliness, 7 and godliness with brotherly
affection, and brotherly affection with love for
everyone.*

*8 The more you grow like this, the more
productive and useful you will be in your
knowledge of our Lord Jesus Christ. 9 But*

those who fail to develop in this way are shortsighted or blind, forgetting that they have been cleansed from their old sins.

This passage lays out the **training process** for a believer—it's the equivalent of a race team fine-tuning a car for peak performance. The more we grow in these qualities, the stronger and more effective we become. But if we ignore them, we become spiritually weak, like a race car running on flat tires.

The Spiritual Sensors: The Fruit of the Spirit

If 2 Peter 1:5-8 is our training program, then **the Fruits of the Spirit** are our **real-time indicators** of how well we're following the Holy Spirit's leading.

"The Holy Spirit produces this kind of fruit in our lives: love, joy, peace, patience, kindness, goodness, faithfulness, gentleness, and self-control." — Galatians 5:22-13

These **nine characteristics** act as our dashboard warning lights:

Love – Are my actions motivated by love, or by selfishness?

Joy – Am I finding joy in God, or am I constantly frustrated and dissatisfied?

Peace – Do I have peace, or am I overwhelmed by worry?

Patience – Am I quick to anger, or do I show patience with others?

Kindness – Do I treat people with kindness, even when they don't deserve it?

Goodness – Are my choices aligned with God's standards of goodness?

Faithfulness – Am I staying committed to God and His Word?

Gentleness – Do I handle situations with gentleness, or am I harsh and aggressive?

Self-control – Do I resist temptation, or do I give in easily to my impulses?

If our thoughts, words, or actions are **not aligned with these fruits**, then we have a **warning signal** that something is off. Just as a race car driver must respond when a sensor indicates a problem, we must also **pause, evaluate, and adjust** when we notice our spiritual indicators warning us of a misalignment.

Adjusting to a New Way of Driving

For some of us, driving with these indicators might feel completely **unnatural** at first. If we've been used to driving our lives with impatience, anger, selfishness, or impulsivity, then learning to follow the Holy Spirit might feel like **rewiring our entire system**.

But here's the truth: **the blessing is in the training**. The goal isn't to suddenly become a perfect driver overnight. The goal is **discipleship**—step by step, day by day, making choices that align us with God's way of living.

Some of us are single, some of us have families, some are in leadership positions, and some are just starting our faith journey. **Each of us faces unique challenges**, but no matter our circumstances, we all need to **evaluate our lives across different areas**:

Family & Relationships – Am I showing love, patience, and kindness to those closest to me?

Social Life – Do I reflect Jesus in the way I interact with others?

Health & Wellness – Am I stewarding my body well?

Career & Finances – Am I making decisions with integrity and trust in God's provision?

Spiritual Life – Am I spending time with God, growing in my knowledge of Him?

Once we identify areas where we are struggling, we can start setting **intentional goals**:

What triggers cause me to deviate from the Fruits of the Spirit?

What Bible verses can I use to renew my mind in those areas?

What daily drills (prayer, worship, Scripture study) can I practice to stay spiritually strong?

Final Lap: Stay in Your Lane

At the end of a Formula 1 race, the winner crosses the finish line, having endured the challenges of the track, the opposition of competitors, and the unpredictability of the race. But every race is different, and every race is won by consistent training, focus, and discipline.

In the same way, our faith journey is about **staying the course, trusting in the Holy Spirit, and producing fruit that reflects Christ in our lives**.

If we stray from the path, we don't have to panic. The Holy Spirit is always there to guide us back, realign our hearts, and strengthen us for the road ahead.

A Formula 1 driver doesn't defeat everything that was against him by **hoping** they will perform well on race day. They **train, study, and prepare** for every possible scenario. Similarly, we don't become spiritually strong by accident. We **train**—we spend time in God's presence, we meditate on His Word, and we allow the Holy Spirit to shape us.

1 Corinthians 9:24-25 reminds us:

> *"Do you not know that in a race all the runners run, but only one gets the prize? Run in such a way as to get the prize. Everyone who competes in the games goes into strict training. They do it to get a crown that will not*

last, but we do it to get a crown that will last forever."

This race of faith is not about perfection, but about **persistence**. The more we train in the Fruits of the Spirit, the more we will reflect **Jesus** in our daily lives that will help us endure any trial or tribulation. And one day, when we cross the finish line, we will hear the words:

"Well done, good and faithful servant." —
Matthew 25:23

Let's keep training. Let's keep growing. Let's stay in the race. **Victory is already ours in Christ.**

Reflection Questions

- Which Fruit of the Spirit do you naturally display the most? Which one do you struggle with the most?

- Think about a recent challenge you faced. How did you respond? Did your response align with the Fruits of the Spirit?

- Are there any "warning lights" flashing in your spiritual life right now? How is the Holy Spirit guiding you to make adjustments?

- In what areas of your life—family, work, friendships—do you need to be more intentional in training yourself spiritually?

- What daily habits can you commit to that will help you grow in the Fruits of the Spirit?

- Who in your life exemplifies the Fruits of the Spirit well? What can you learn from them?

- How can you rely more on the Holy Spirit's guidance rather than your own strength in this race of faith?

Closing Prayer

Heavenly Father,

Thank You for calling me to run this race of faith. I know I cannot do it on my own, so I surrender my heart to You. Holy Spirit, train me, shape me, and guide me in every step. Help me to bear the Fruits of the Spirit—let my life overflow with love, joy, peace, patience, kindness, goodness, faithfulness, gentleness, and self-control.

When I drift off course, remind me of Your truth. When I feel weak, strengthen me with Your grace. When I face obstacles, help me persevere with faith. Lord, I don't just want to be a believer in name—I want to be an athlete of faith, running with endurance, reflecting Jesus in all I do.

Help me to stay close to You, to hear Your voice clearly, and to live a life that brings You glory. Thank You for being my Coach, my Strength, and my Victory.

*In Jesus' name, **Amen.***

Chapter 7

Fitness Test

Holy Spirit's VO2 Max Check

In the world of elite athletics, fitness is not measured by guesswork—it's tested. One of the most important assessments for endurance athletes is the **VO2 max test**, which measures how efficiently their bodies use oxygen. It determines their current fitness level and reveals what kind of training they need to improve. Without this data, an athlete might train the wrong way, pushing too hard in one area while neglecting another, leading to burnout or weakness.

Our faith is no different. Just as oxygen fuels the athlete, **the breath of God—His living Word—fuels us**. The Holy Spirit, our divine Coach, is constantly assessing our **spiritual fitness**, revealing where we are strong and where we need to grow. His diagnostic tool? **The Fruit of the Spirit.**

Galatians 5:22-23 gives us **nine indicators** of a Spirit-led life:

> *"The Holy Spirit produces this kind of fruit in our lives: love, joy, peace, patience, kindness, goodness, faithfulness, gentleness, and self-control."*

These are more than just good character traits; they are the signs of a well-conditioned spiritual life. Just like an athlete's test results show where they need more endurance or strength, **each Fruit of the Spirit is a checkpoint revealing how deeply we are relying on the Holy Spirit or where we may be spiritually weak**.

- **Is my love unconditional, or does it depend on circumstances?**

- **Do I have joy, or am I constantly discouraged?**

- **Am I walking in peace, or am I weighed down by anxiety?**

- **Do I have patience, or do I easily lose my temper?**

These are not questions to condemn us but to **guide us toward the right training program**. Therefore, this next section will take us deeper into each Fruit of the Spirit, helping us understand:

- **How each fruit strengthens us against the enemy's traps**

- **What daily drills we can do to cultivate spiritual endurance**

- **How to measure our progress and adjust when we fall short**

Remember, the goal is not perfection but **persistence**. The Holy Spirit is ready to train you—are you ready to take the test?

Chapter 8

Joy

Your Inner Fuel

I n the world of sports, athletes often speak of "the zone"—a place where everything clicks, and performance seems effortless. For the Christian, joy is like entering that zone of spiritual freedom, where we are fully aware of God's presence and our hearts align with His purposes. True joy doesn't come from our circumstances or accomplishments but from the confidence that we are beloved children of a faithful Father. It's a joy that can thrive in all conditions, lifting us when life feels heavy. In this chapter, we'll explore how joy, as a fruit of the Spirit, serves as a source of strength, peace, and endurance in the Christian life, helping us run our race with perseverance and purpose.

Biblical Insight: Joy as the Strength for the Journey

In his letter to the Philippians, Paul encourages us in Philippians 4:4 to:

> *"Rejoice in the Lord always"*

This isn't a suggestion—it's a command. Joy is not merely an emotion we feel; it's a choice we make. It is the fruit of the Holy Spirit, an evidence of our relationship with God that goes beyond surface happiness.

The joy that comes from the Lord is unique—it's not circumstantial. The joy we experience as believers is anchored in our identity in Christ. Jesus himself tells us in John 15:11:

> *"I have told you this so that my joy may be in you and that your joy may be complete."*

His joy is not dependent on the ups and downs of life but on His constant presence with us. The joy we experience in Him strengthens our spirits, enabling us to endure hardships, face challenges, and remain steadfast in our faith.

Nehemiah 8:10 declares:

"The joy of the Lord is your strength."

This verse shows us that joy is not just a nice feeling—it is a source of power. When we tap into God's joy, we are equipped to face whatever comes our way with strength and courage. The trials we encounter are part of the process, refining us, teaching us to depend on God's strength, and producing fruit that reflects His goodness.

Practical Wisdom: How Joy Strengthens Our Faith

It Refines Our Focus

Joy shifts our focus. When we rejoice in the Lord, we redirect our attention away from our circumstances and onto God's promises. It's easy to get bogged down by worries, stresses, and disappointments. But when we choose joy, we remind ourselves of God's faithfulness and goodness, even in the midst of trials. Joy helps us see the bigger picture, one that is filled with hope and possibility.

In Hebrews 12:2, we are told to:

> *"fix our eyes on Jesus, the author and perfecter of faith."*

As we rejoice in Him, we remember that He is our ultimate source of joy, and we can draw strength from His perfect example of perseverance. He endured the cross for the joy set before Him (Hebrews 12:2), showing us that joy is the fuel that keeps us moving forward, even when the road gets tough.

It Replaces Anxiety

Joy doesn't just make us feel good—it brings peace. Jesus encourages us in Matthew 6:34:

> *"So don't worry about tomorrow, for tomorrow will bring its own worries. Today's trouble is enough for today."*

When we trust God and rejoice in His control over our lives, we release the anxiety that weighs us down.

As we cultivate joy, we are reminded that God holds our future in His hands. Trusting in His perfect timing and provision allows us to live free of the worries that often rob us of peace. Instead of being consumed by what might happen tomorrow, joy grounds us in the present moment, filling us with peace and confidence in God's plans.

It Cultivates Gratitude

Gratitude is a natural byproduct of joy. When we experience joy, it prompts us to reflect on all that God has done for us. It's easy to focus on what we don't have, but joy helps us recognize the countless blessings that surround us.

1 Thessalonians 5:16-18 encourages us:

> *"Rejoice always, pray continually, give thanks in all circumstances."*

Gratitude deepens our experience of joy. As we reflect on all that God has done, we are drawn into deeper worship and thanksgiving. Joy helps us cultivate a heart of gratitude that shifts our perspective, allowing us to see God's goodness in every season.

How to Cultivate Joy Through Life's Refining Process

Stay Connected to Christ

Just as an athlete must train consistently to remain in peak condition, we must stay connected to the source of our joy—Jesus Christ. Spend time in prayer, worship, and Scripture to nurture your relationship with Him. The more we draw near to God, the more His joy will fill our hearts.

John 15:5 reminds us:

> "I am the vine; you are the branches. If you remain in me and I in you, you will bear much fruit."

When we remain in Christ, we experience the fullness of His joy. We are also equipped to face the challenges that come our way, knowing that He is with us every step of the way.

Surrender to His Refining Process

Embrace the refining process that God is taking you through. Joy is often most profound in the midst of hardship because it's in those moments that we truly experience God's presence. Instead of avoiding challenges, see them as opportunities for growth. God's refining work may be difficult, but it produces in us a deeper joy that we wouldn't otherwise experience.

James 1:2-4 teaches us:

> *"Consider it pure joy, my brothers and sisters, whenever you face trials of many kinds, because you know that the testing of your faith produces perseverance."*

Trials are not just obstacles—they are tools in God's hands to shape us into the people He desires us to be.

Celebrate Small Wins

Just as an athlete celebrates small victories along the

way, take time to celebrate the moments of joy that God provides. Acknowledge the blessings, no matter how small, and give thanks for them. Each step of growth in your faith is worth rejoicing over.

Psalm 118:24 says:

> *"This is the day the Lord has made; let us rejoice and be glad in it."*

Every day is an opportunity to rejoice in God's goodness, even if the day didn't go as planned.

Real-Life Application: Living Out Joy in Every Situation

Imagine facing a difficult situation at work, school, or home. Instead of focusing on frustration, choose joy by trusting that God is using the challenge to refine you and make you stronger. Look for ways to be a source of joy to others—through a kind word, a smile, or encouragement—even in hard times.

Here are some practical ways to live out joy:

When faced with disappointment, remind yourself

that God is in control and using the situation for your good.

Share a testimony of God's faithfulness to encourage someone else.

Take time to reflect on and celebrate the blessings God has placed in your life.

Reflection Prompts

- What areas of your life are currently challenging your joy? How can you trust God's refining process in those situations?

- When was the last time you rejoiced in God's goodness? How can you make space for more joy in your life?

- How can you encourage others to find joy and strength in God, even during difficult times?

Action Steps

Gratitude Journal: Write down three things you're thankful for each day, focusing on how God is working in your life.

Practice Rejoicing: Set aside time daily to praise God for His goodness through song, prayer, or reflection.

Share Joy: Tell someone how God has brought joy into your life and encourage them to seek His joy as well.

Closing Prayer

Father, thank You for the joy that You provide, a joy that transcends our circumstances and fills us with strength. Help us to remain connected to You, to trust Your refining process, and to celebrate the blessings You bring into our lives. May Your joy become the fuel for our faith, empowering us to face life's challenges with perseverance and peace. Fill our hearts with joy so that we can share it with others and bring glory to Your name. In Jesus' name, **Amen.**

Chapter 9

Peace I

Storm Rider

The story of Jesus sleeping during the storm (Mark 4:35-41) is one of the most vivid examples of peace in action. Imagine the scene: the disciples, many of whom were experienced fishermen, are overwhelmed by the ferocity of the storm. They wake Jesus with desperation, shouting,

"Teacher, don't you care if we drown?"

At this moment, Jesus wakes up, calms the storm with His words, and then turns to the disciples with a challenge:

"Why are you so afraid? Do you still have no faith?"

This simple yet profound interaction reveals vital lessons for those training as Athletes of Faith:

Jesus' Peace Is Rooted in Faith

While the storm raged, Jesus slept peacefully because His faith was unshakable. His trust in the Father's sovereignty allowed Him to rest, even when circumstances seemed dire. He knew that God's plan would prevail no matter how chaotic the scene around Him appeared. As Athletes of Faith, our peace must be anchored in the same unshakable confidence that God is in control. Peace is not the absence of storms, but the presence of faith in God's perfect purpose within them.

Choose Faith Over Fear

Jesus' response to the disciples' fear isn't merely a rebuke—it's an invitation to grow. He doesn't just want us to marvel at His power to calm the storm; He wants us to trust Him so deeply that we can remain calm in the storm. The question isn't whether storms will come—they will—but whether we will face them with faith or fear.

Fear can cause us to panic, lose focus, or even paralyze us. Faith, on the other hand, enables us to stay grounded and hopeful, trusting in the bigger picture. Faith and peace are inseparable. The more we choose to trust God in the midst of difficulty, the more peace we experience—peace that transcends understanding and holds us steady through the storm.

Our Choice in Faith: Circling or Advancing?

The Israelites' journey in the wilderness offers another powerful illustration of the difference between fear-driven faith and bold trust in God. Despite God's daily provision of manna and His constant presence, the Israelites lacked the faith to step into the Promised Land. They wandered for 40 years, circling the same terrain, because they couldn't move past their fears. Fear held them back from the promises God had made to them.

Contrast this with Joshua and Caleb, who boldly declared in Numbers 14:9:

"The Lord is with us. Do not be afraid"

Their unwavering trust in God's faithfulness allowed them to move forward, leading the next generation into the Promised Land. Their faith wasn't just in God's power—it was in His love and care for them, enabling them to advance rather than retreat.

As Athletes of Faith, we must ask ourselves: Will we wander in circles, stuck in fear and doubt, avoiding the storms of life and the challenges that come with them? Or will we train our faith, becoming bold and courageous like Joshua, knowing that God is with us every step of the way?

The shoes of peace equip us to move forward, not just stand still. They give us the confidence to take new ground, knowing that God has already gone before us. Peace is the anchor that steadies us, even as the waves rise and the winds blow. It is the deep assurance that, with God, we will not only survive the storms but emerge stronger on the other side.

Becoming a Storm Rider

An Athlete of Faith doesn't seek to avoid storms but learns to ride them with grace and strength. Just as athletes don't cancel a race because of rain, we must be prepared to compete regardless of life's challenges. The storms of life are inevitable, but they don't define us—they refine us.

The Apostle Peter experienced this firsthand when he walked on water (Matthew 14:22-33). At first, his focus on Jesus allowed him to do the impossible—walk on the waves. But when he shifted his attention to the wind and waves, fear took over, and he began to sink. Jesus' outstretched hand reminds us that His grace is always available to lift us when we falter.

We may not always walk on water, but we can learn to ride the waves with peace, confidence, and perseverance. The shoes of peace aren't just armor—they're also tools for navigating life's challenges. Imagine them as surfboards of faith, enabling us to ride the waves instead of being overwhelmed by them. When storms arise, we don't pray for them to stop; we pray for the wisdom, grace, and endurance to navigate through them.

Practical Steps to Become a Storm Rider

Shift Your Perspective: Instead of asking God to calm every storm, ask Him to strengthen your faith.

Meditate on Jesus' words: "Take heart; it is I. Do not be afraid" (Matthew 14:27). Your focus must shift from the size of the storm to the greatness of your Savior.

Daily Faith Training: Strengthen your trust in God by recalling past victories. Journal moments when God provided, guided, or protected you. Let these testimonies fuel your confidence when new challenges arise.

Embrace Challenges: View trials as opportunities to grow your spiritual endurance. James 1:2-4 reminds us, "Consider it pure joy whenever you face trials of many kinds, because you know that the testing of your faith produces perseverance." Storms are not obstacles to avoid but opportunities to grow and trust more deeply.

Stay Focused on Jesus: Like Peter, keep your eyes on Jesus, especially when the waves of life feel overwhelming. Worship, prayer, and Scripture are your lifelines—keep them close. When you focus on Him, the storms around you lose their power to shake your peace.

Reflection Prompts

- In what areas of your life are you asking God to calm the storm instead of asking Him to grow your faith?

- How can you prepare yourself spiritually to become a storm rider?

- What steps can you take today to trust God more deeply, even when the waves rise?

Action Steps

Gratitude Journal: Write down three things you're thankful for each day, focusing on how God is working in your life.

Practice Rejoicing: Set aside time daily to praise God for His goodness through song, prayer, or reflection.

Share Peace: Tell someone how God has brought peace into your life and encourage them to seek His peace, especially in difficult times.

Closing Prayer

Lord Jesus, thank You for being my peace in the storm. Teach me to trust You fully, even when life feels overwhelming. Equip me with the shoes of peace, so I can stand firm and move forward, no matter the challenges I face. Help me to shift my focus from fear to faith, knowing that You are always with me. May I become a storm rider, walking boldly on the waves of life through Your grace and strength. In Your name, **Amen.**

Chapter 10

Peace II

The Shoes of Peace

Active Preparation and Traction in Trials

Every athlete knows that their performance is the result of rigorous preparation. The same is true for us when it comes to peace—it is not merely the absence of conflict or chaos, but a readiness that is deeply rooted in trust and reliance on God. When Paul speaks about the "shoes of peace" in Ephesians 6:15, he links them to the "gospel of peace." This gospel doesn't just bring tranquility; it equips us to move forward confidently, no matter what battlefield we face.

Foundation of Peace

Just as athletes train their bodies to perform under

pressure, we must condition our hearts through Scripture, prayer, and worship. Peace begins by knowing who God is and trusting His promises. This foundational knowledge equips us with the stability we need to navigate life's storms. Psalm 119:165 reminds us:

> *"Great peace have those who love your law,*
> *and nothing can make them stumble."*

When we prepare by anchoring ourselves in God's truth, we can walk through life with unwavering confidence, unaffected by the shifting circumstances around us.

Traction in Trials

Shoes are not just about comfort—they provide traction, helping athletes stay balanced on uneven terrain. Similarly, God's peace gives us the traction we need when the enemy tries to shake our faith. The Apostle Paul writes in Philippians 4:7:

> *"And the peace of God, which surpasses all*

*understanding, will guard your hearts and
your minds in Christ Jesus."*

Peace is not something we simply stumble into—it
is the result of daily preparation and faithfulness.
Without this preparation, fear and anxiety will
dominate. But when we stay rooted in God's Word and
trust Him, His peace guards us, especially when the
storm rages.

Peace Is Active, Not Passive

Jesus demonstrated that peace is not a passive state;
it is a powerful force that allows us to face challenges
with strength. When He rebuked the storm in Mark
4:39, He showed that peace comes with authority.
That same authority is available to us when we abide
in Him.

Overcoming Fear: Fear is one of the enemy's favorite
tools, but peace is our weapon to overcome it. Isaiah
41:10 reminds us:

> *"Do not fear, for I am with you; do not be
> dismayed, for I am your God."*

Relying on Faith, Not Circumstances: Jesus challenged His disciples' faith in the storm, asking, "Do you still have no faith?" (Mark 4:40). This question pushes us to trust not in what we see, but in who God is. The peace of an experienced sailor doesn't come from the calmness of the sea—it comes from knowing they are prepared for the storm.

Practical Steps to Wear the Shoes of Peace

Peace doesn't come naturally; it requires daily preparation. Here are practical steps to equip yourself with the shoes of peace:

Anchor in the Word: Meditate on Scriptures that emphasize God's peace and promises. Let them be your foundation. Suggested verses: John 14:27, Colossians 3:15, Isaiah 26:3.

Prayer as Preparation: Make prayer your daily warm-up. Thank God for His peace and ask for His guidance in everything you do. Prayer is a vital part of your preparation.

Cultivate Calmness: Practice remaining calm during minor inconveniences. Use these moments as training for greater storms.

Community Support: Surround yourself with believers who model peace in action. Lean on the Body of Christ for encouragement and strength.

Faith-Fueled Action: Step boldly into challenges, knowing that God's peace has equipped you for victory. Confidence in God's preparation enables us to press forward, even in tough moments.

Reflection Prompts

- Are there areas in your life where you've been running without your "shoes of peace"?

- How can you practice resting in God's promises instead of striving in your own strength?

- Think of a recent storm in your life. How would wearing the shoes of peace have changed your response or perspective?

Closing Prayer

Heavenly Father,
Thank You for the gift of peace that surpasses all
understanding. Help me to put on the shoes of peace

every day, anchoring my life in Your truth and promises. Teach me to trust You in the storms, to move forward in faith, and to be a bearer of peace in a world full of chaos. Equip me to stand firm against the enemy's schemes and to reflect Your love and grace in all I do. In Jesus' name, **Amen.**

Chapter 11

Rest in the Race

The Power of Recovery

E lite athletes understand that rest is not a luxury—it's a necessity. They follow strategic recovery plans, knowing that without intentional rest, their performance will suffer, and they risk burnout or injury.

The same is true for our spiritual race. Many believers push themselves relentlessly, equating busyness with faithfulness. But without resting in God, we grow weary, spiritually exhausted, and vulnerable to discouragement. That's why God calls us to rest—not as an excuse for laziness, but as a strategy for endurance.

Just as an athlete's ice bath soothes sore muscles, God's Word is our cooling relief when we are overwhelmed by life's struggles. When we soak in

Scripture, it refreshes our weary souls and renews our strength. Just as an athlete enters a recovery chamber, our prayer time becomes our place of restoration—where the Holy Spirit heals our hearts, refocuses our minds, and prepares us for the next challenge.

Jesus Himself modeled this rhythm. Though He carried the weight of the world, He often withdrew to quiet places to pray (Luke 5:16). He taught that rest is not a weakness, but a sign of wisdom and trust in God's provision:

> *"Come to me, all you who are weary*
> *and burdened, and I will give you rest."* —
> Matthew 11:28

If we want to run our spiritual race well, we must learn the discipline of rest. Just as an athlete recovers to perform at their peak, we must learn to rest in God to fulfill our calling. The key to endurance is not just in how hard we push—but in how well we recover.

Practical Wisdom: Why We Struggle to Rest

Many of us resist rest for one of these reasons:

We equate busyness with productivity. We believe we must be constantly doing something to make progress.

We fear falling behind. Slowing down feels like missing opportunities or failing in responsibilities.

We don't trust God's provision. We rely on our own efforts instead of believing that God will sustain us.

We are addicted to distractions. Instead of true rest, we fill our time with entertainment, social media, and noise that do not refresh our souls.

We don't understand the power of spiritual rest. We fail to realize that time with God renews us more than anything else.

Recognizing these struggles allows us to correct our mindset and embrace rest as God intended.

Real-Life Application: How to Experience True Rest

Rest is not merely stopping activity; it's engaging in the right kind of recovery. Here are four ways we can experience true rest:

1. Rest in God's Word (The Ice Bath for Your Soul)

Just as an athlete steps into an ice bath to reduce inflammation, we can immerse ourselves in God's Word to ease our spiritual burdens. Scripture refreshes us and brings healing to our tired souls.

Application: Set aside 15 minutes daily to read and reflect on a passage of Scripture, allowing God's Word to wash over you.

2. Rest in Prayer (The Recovery Chamber)

Athletes use recovery chambers to heal faster. Likewise, prayer is our spiritual recovery chamber. When we spend time with God, He replenishes our strength, removes fear, and gives us clarity.

Application: Take moments throughout the day to pause, breathe, and connect with God—whether in deep prayer or simply acknowledging His presence.

3. Rest in Sabbath (The Scheduled Recovery Day)

Athletes schedule rest days into their training because they know it's essential for long-term endurance. God commanded the Sabbath as a day of rest to remind us that He is our provider and we don't have to strive constantly.

Application: Dedicate one day a week to disconnect from work, stress, and distractions, focusing on worship, reflection, and family.

4. Rest in Fellowship (Team Recovery)

Even in sports, athletes don't recover alone—they have trainers, coaches, and teammates to support them. Likewise, God designed us to rest and be encouraged in community.

Application: Surround yourself with believers who uplift you and remind you of God's promises. Join a small group, attend a Bible study, or spend time with encouraging friends.

Reflection Prompts

Take a moment to reflect on the following questions:

- Where in my life do I feel most exhausted?

- Do I trust God enough to rest, or do I feel like everything depends on me?

- How can I build more intentional moments of spiritual rest in my daily routine?

- What Scriptures can I meditate on when I feel overwhelmed?

- Who in my life encourages me to rest in God? How can I connect with them more?

Write down your thoughts and ask God to guide you toward a healthier rhythm of rest.

Action Steps

Set a daily Scripture time – Even if it's just 15 minutes, commit to soaking in God's Word.

Schedule prayer breaks – Take short moments throughout your day to breathe, pray, and surrender your burdens to God.

Honor the Sabbath – Dedicate one day a week to rest and worship.

Limit distractions – Identify activities that drain you (e.g., excessive social media, overworking) and replace them with life-giving habits.

Seek godly community – Find a group of believers who encourage you to rest in Christ.

Final Encouragement: Resting is Winning

Athletes who fail to rest end up injured, exhausted, and unable to finish their race. The same is true for believers. If we don't learn to rest in God, we will burn out before fulfilling our purpose.

Rest is not a sign of weakness—it is a sign of trust. It is the confidence that God is working even when we are still. It is the assurance that we don't have to strive in our own strength, because His grace is enough.

So as we run our race, let's remember: **resting is not quitting. Resting is winning.**

Closing Prayer

Heavenly Father,
Thank You for reminding me that rest is a gift, not a weakness. I confess that I often try to do everything in my own strength and forget to come to You for refreshment. Teach me to rest in Your presence, to trust that You are in control, and to embrace the rhythm of recovery You have designed for me. Renew my strength, restore my soul, and help me to run my race with endurance.
In Jesus' name, **Amen.**

Chapter 12

Patience

The Endurance Test

The Athlete's Battle with Time

Imagine a long-distance runner preparing for a marathon. The race is not won in the first few strides—it's an endurance test. In the early miles, they feel strong, full of energy, and tempted to sprint ahead. But seasoned runners know better. They pace themselves, understanding that a race is lost when impatience takes over. Go too fast too soon, and exhaustion will set in before the finish line. Hold steady, endure the burning muscles, and victory is within reach.

Every great athlete understands that success doesn't happen overnight. Strength isn't built in a day, endurance isn't gained in a week, and championships aren't won in a single season. It takes years of consistent training, discipline, and, most of all—patience.

Patience is the unseen force behind every victory. It's what keeps a runner moving when progress feels slow. It's what allows a weightlifter to endure thousands of painful reps before seeing results. It's what makes a soccer player practice the same drill over and over until it becomes second nature.

Athletes know that rushing leads to injury. A runner who pushes too hard too soon will pull a muscle. A lifter who increases weight too quickly will strain a joint. Impatience in training can destroy an athlete's future. That's why patience is not just a virtue—it's a survival skill.

The same is true in our spiritual race. We often want instant results—immediate breakthroughs, overnight growth, quick answers to our prayers. But God's way is different. He develops us through time, testing, and endurance.

This is why Scripture tells us:

"But those who wait on the LORD shall renew their strength; they shall mount up with wings like eagles, they shall run and not be weary, they shall walk and not faint." — Isaiah 40:31

Just as an athlete trusts the process of training, we must trust God's timing in our lives. Spiritual strength is built through seasons of waiting, perseverance, and unwavering faith. Patience isn't passive—it's active endurance.

Biblical Insight: Patience as Endurance

Patience is more than just waiting—it's how we wait. James 5:7-8 illustrates this beautifully:

"Be patient, then, brothers and sisters, until the Lord's coming. See how the farmer waits for the land to yield its valuable crop, patiently waiting for the autumn and spring rains. You too, be patient and stand firm, because the Lord's coming is near."

Patience is closely tied to trust in God's timing. Jesus

exemplified this in His ministry, often withdrawing to pray and waiting on the Father's direction. Even when His disciples urged immediate action, Jesus moved in perfect alignment with God's plan, showing us the importance of patience in fulfilling our purpose.

Practical Wisdom: Cultivating Patience

To grow in patience, we must train our hearts to persevere through life's challenges:

Embrace God's Timing
Ecclesiastes 3:1 reminds us that there is a season for everything. Trusting God's timing frees us from anxiety and impatience.

Shift Your Perspective
Romans 8:28 assures us that God works all things together for good. Viewing delays and challenges as opportunities for growth can transform frustration into faith.

Practice Self-Control
Proverbs 14:29 teaches, *"Whoever is patient has great understanding, but one who is quick-tempered displays folly."* Patience requires us to resist impulsive reactions and lean into God's wisdom.

Real-Life Application: Patience in Action

Patience manifests in different areas of our lives:

In Relationships: Patience helps us navigate conflicts with grace, giving others the space to grow and change.

In Trials: Enduring hardship with a steadfast heart strengthens our faith and deepens our reliance on God.

In Ministry: Waiting for God's promises to unfold teaches us humility and dependence on His power.

For example, a parent showing patience with a rebellious child reflects God's own long-suffering love for us. A leader patiently mentoring a struggling team member mirrors Christ's dedication to His disciples. Each act of patience becomes a testimony of God's grace at work in us.

Reflection Prompts

- How do you typically respond to delays or unmet expectations?

- Can you identify an area in your life where God is teaching you patience?

- How has patience—or the lack of it—impacted your relationships or spiritual growth?

Action Steps: Training in Patience

Memorize a Key Verse: Choose a scripture about patience, such as Galatians 6:9: *"Let us not become weary in doing good, for at the proper time we will reap a harvest if we do not give up."* Repeat it whenever you feel impatient.

Set a "Pause" Goal: The next time you feel frustrated or rushed, pause for five seconds before reacting. Use this time to pray or reflect on God's timing.

Create a Gratitude List: Write down ways God has been faithful in your life. Reflecting on His past provision can renew your patience for current challenges.

Final Encouragement: Patience Produces Champions

Great athletes don't become champions overnight. They train, endure, and trust the process.

The same is true for spiritual champions. Patience is the bridge between where you are now and where God is taking you. If you stay faithful, if you trust His timing, if you keep going even when it's hard—you will see His promises fulfilled.

> *"Let us run with endurance the race set before us, keeping our eyes on Jesus, the author and perfecter of our faith."* — Hebrews 12:1-2

Stay in the race. Patience isn't delay—it's preparation.

Closing Prayer

Dear Jesus, Lord of Patience, thank You for Your long-suffering love and for the countless times You have waited on me to grow. Teach me to trust in Your perfect timing and to persevere through life's delays with faith and grace. Help me to see waiting as an opportunity *to deepen my relationship with You and to reflect Your character in my responses to others. Strengthen me to endure trials with joy and to remain steadfast in the race of faith. In Jesus' name, **Amen.***

Chapter 13

Kindness

Legacy over Results

In 1968, during the Olympic Games in Mexico City, an extraordinary act of kindness and sportsmanship left an impact that transcended generations. John Stephen Akhwari, a marathon runner from Tanzania, finished his race long after the stadium had emptied. He had fallen earlier in the race, dislocating his knee and suffering deep cuts, yet he refused to quit. As he limped across the finish line, when asked why he had continued despite the pain, he simply replied:

"My country did not send me 5,000 miles to start the race; they sent me to finish the race."

His perseverance was inspiring, but the kindness he received along the way was just as powerful.

Spectators, officials, and fellow athletes encouraged him, offering water, medical aid, and applause as he pressed on. He did not win a medal that day, but his legacy of determination and the kindness shown to him became a lasting symbol of what truly matters in sports—and in life.

Kindness in competition may seem like a contradiction, but history shows us that the greatest athletes are not only measured by their victories but by the way they uplift others. Whether it's a tennis player conceding a point they know was wrongly awarded or a soccer player helping an injured opponent instead of taking advantage, these moments of kindness define true champions. They remind us that being great is not just about personal success—it's about how we use our platform to bring kindness and integrity into the world.

As followers of Christ, we are called to run our race with kindness, reflecting God's love in every situation. The Bible reminds us:

> *"Be kind to one another, tenderhearted,*
> *forgiving one another, as God in Christ*

forgave you." — Ephesians 4:32

Kindness: Strength, Not Weakness

Many mistake kindness for weakness, but in reality, it requires tremendous strength. It takes courage to be kind when others are rude, patience to remain gentle under pressure, and faith to forgive when wronged. Just as athletes train their bodies for competition, we must train our hearts to be kind, even in the most competitive and high-stakes moments.

Biblical Insight: The Essence of Kindness

Kindness is at the core of God's character. *Titus 3:4-5 reminds us:*

> *"But when the kindness and love of God our Savior appeared, He saved us, not because of righteous things we had done, but because of His mercy."*

Jesus embodied kindness in every aspect of His ministry—healing the sick, feeding the hungry, and showing mercy to those society had rejected. His kindness was never passive; it was bold, intentional, and transformative. As Paul instructs in Colossians 3:12, we are to clothe ourselves with kindness as part of our identity in Christ. This is not just a suggestion—it's essential for those who seek to reflect God's love in a world desperately in need of it.

Practical Wisdom: Cultivating Kindness

Many people view kindness as an optional trait, but it is actually a spiritual muscle that must be strengthened daily. Here's why kindness is crucial:

Kindness reflects Christ – Jesus was powerful, but He led with compassion, grace, and mercy.

Kindness strengthens relationships – It builds trust, unity, and respect in teams, friendships, and families.

Kindness turns enemies into allies – A gentle response can defuse conflict and open hearts (Proverbs 15:1).

Kindness brings healing – Encouraging words and acts of love can restore broken people.

Kindness multiplies – When you show kindness, it spreads—people remember it and pass it on.

Great athletes don't just compete—they inspire others. And the greatest impact you can have is not just in winning but in how you treat those around you.

Real-Life Application: Kindness in Action

Kindness can transform ordinary interactions into extraordinary opportunities to reflect Christ. Here are a few examples:

At Work: A colleague struggling with a heavy workload may benefit from your help or encouragement.

In Family: Kind words and gestures can heal conflicts and strengthen relationships.

In the Community: Volunteering at a shelter, donating to those in need, or even holding the door for someone can spread God's love.

One of the most powerful biblical examples of kindness in action is the story of the Good Samaritan (Luke 10:25-37). Despite cultural and social divisions, the Samaritan cared for a stranger in need. His kindness was inconvenient and costly, but it demonstrated the selfless love of God.

Reflection Prompts

Take a moment to reflect:

- How do I treat people when I'm frustrated or under pressure?

- Have I ever experienced life-changing kindness from someone else?

- Are my words and actions building people up or tearing them down?

- How can I be more intentional about showing kindness daily?

- What does Jesus' kindness teach me about how I should live?

Write down your thoughts and let God speak to your heart.

Action Steps: Practicing Kindness Daily

Pray for a Kind Heart: Ask God to reveal opportunities to show kindness and to soften your heart toward others.

Perform One Act of Kindness Daily: Whether it's offering a compliment, sending a kind message, or lending a helping hand, commit to making kindness a habit.

Forgive Freely: Sometimes, the greatest act of kindness is letting go of a grudge and offering forgiveness.

Run your race with strength, but always choose kindness along the way. It's not just about winning—it's about who you become in the process.

Closing Prayer

Lord of Compassion,

Thank You for Your endless kindness toward me. Help me to reflect that same kindness to others, even when it's inconvenient or undeserved. Teach me to see others through Your eyes and to respond with love and grace. May my actions and words bring encouragement and hope, pointing others to You. Equip me to be a vessel of Your kindness in every area of my life.

In Jesus' name, ***Amen.***

Chapter 14

Goodness

A Beacon in the Darkness

*"You are the light of the world—like a city on a hilltop that cannot be hidden. No one lights a lamp and then puts it under a basket. Instead, a lamp is placed on a stand, where it gives light to everyone in the house. In the same way, **let your good deeds shine out for all to see, so that everyone will praise your heavenly Father.** — Mathew 5:14-16*

As athletes of faith, we are not just training for physical strength or moral achievements. We are training our hearts, minds, and souls to reflect God's goodness in everything we do. Goodness is not simply about doing good deeds; it is about becoming a person of excellence, integrity, and holiness through the transformative power of the Holy Spirit.

A Tale of Two Players: Talent vs. True Goodness

In the world of soccer, many players are celebrated for their skills, goals, and trophies. Their talent shines under the stadium lights, and their names echo in the chants of millions of fans. But there is a difference between using success for personal glory and using it to bless others.

One example of true goodness in sports is **Sadio Mané**. A world-class footballer, a Champions League winner, and a hero for Senegal, Mané is not only known for his skill but also for his heart. Instead of chasing fame and fortune, he has dedicated his wealth and influence to serving others, building hospitals, schools, and infrastructure in his home village. Rather than living extravagantly, he chooses to live modestly, using his resources to bless those in need. His life reflects the heart of goodness—not just appearing good, but actively being a light in the world.

In contrast, there are footballers who have achieved the same success but use their fame to enrich themselves, indulging in luxuries while ignoring the suffering around them. They may donate occasionally or say the right things in interviews, but their actions reveal where their hearts truly lie.

This mirrors the **parable of the Good Samaritan** (Luke 10:25-37). A priest and a Levite—figures expected to embody righteousness—ignored a wounded man, while a Samaritan, an outsider, stopped to help. His goodness was not in his title but in his actions.

Just like in football, some players appear good but act selfishly, while others quietly serve and uplift others. God does not call us to simply look good in front of others—He calls us to **be the light and salt of the world** (Matthew 5:13-16).

God's Goodness as Our Foundation

When we say, "God is good all the time," we are not claiming life is always easy or fair. Instead, we are declaring a truth: **God's nature is inherently good**, and He works all things together for our good (Romans 8:28). His goodness is seen in His love, mercy, justice, forgiveness, and holiness.

This goodness is the foundation of our training as athletes of faith. Just as a coach provides guidance, correction, and encouragement, **God's goodness equips us** to grow spiritually and emotionally. Psalm 34:8 invites us to:

> *"taste and see that the Lord is good."*

Experiencing His goodness firsthand transforms how we live and interact with others.

But here's the key: God doesn't just want us to experience His goodness—**He wants us to reflect it**. Like Jesus, who demonstrated perfect goodness in His ministry, we are called to be lights in the world, showing others what it means to live a life rooted in God's love and truth.

True Goodness vs. Superficial Goodness

In a world that rewards appearances, it is tempting to settle for superficial goodness—doing good deeds for praise or self-promotion. But as Galatians 6:9 reminds us:

*"Let us not grow weary of doing good, for in
due season we will reap, if we do not give up."*

Superficial goodness seeks recognition and approval.
It thrives on applause and social status.
True goodness is selfless, grounded in God's grace,
and focused on serving others.

God's goodness transforms us from the inside out,
shaping our thoughts, motives, and actions. As James
1:17 says:

*"Every good and perfect gift is from above,
coming down from the Father of lights."*

Our goodness is not something we manufacture; it is
a **reflection of God's work in us**.

How to Train in Goodness

Just like any athletic discipline, developing the fruit
of goodness requires **intentionality and practice**.
Here's how we can grow in this vital aspect of our faith
journey:

Stop and Reflect Before Acting

Much like an athlete analyzing their next move, pause before making decisions. Ask yourself:

- Is this action aligned with God's standards or the world's?

- Am I motivated by love and righteousness, or by a desire to impress others?

- Would God consider this thought, word, or action "good"?

Reflection helps us align our intentions with God's truth, ensuring our actions flow from a place of **genuine goodness**.

Pray for Guidance

Prayer is our lifeline to God, the ultimate source of goodness. Through prayer, we can discern what is truly good and resist the false standards of the world. St. Augustine's words are a powerful reminder: **"You have made us for yourself, O Lord, and our hearts are restless until they find their rest in You."**

Pray for **God's wisdom** to guide your choices and for His Spirit to strengthen your commitment to goodness, even when it's challenging.

Trust in God's Goodness

As athletes of faith, we must trust that **God's goodness is greater than any challenge or setback**. He knows what is best for us, even when circumstances seem unfair or painful. Hebrews 12:2 encourages us to **fix our eyes on Jesus**, "the pioneer and perfecter of our faith," who endured the cross for the joy set before Him.

Trusting in God's goodness enables us to **persevere with hope and confidence**, knowing He is working in and through us.

Choose Life Over Death

Training in goodness means consistently choosing **life over the destructive forces of sin**. This involves turning away from harmful habits, toxic influences, and sinful behaviors that hinder our spiritual growth. Deuteronomy 30:19 reminds us:

"I have set before you life and death, blessings and curses. Now choose life, so that you and your children may live."

Just as an athlete pushes through challenges to reach their goals, we must actively **pursue holiness**, even when it means sacrificing worldly success or comfort. By choosing life—the life that comes from God—we grow in goodness and reflect His character more fully.

Cultivate Virtue

Goodness grows alongside other virtues such as **kindness, patience, and humility**. Surround yourself with people who inspire and challenge you to live a virtuous life. Engage in **Scripture, worship, and meaningful conversations** that deepen your understanding of God's character.

The Legacy of Goodness

Jesus is the **ultimate example of goodness**. He lived a life of perfect obedience, compassion, and selflessness, setting a standard for us to follow. As we grow in goodness, we reflect His light in a world desperate for hope and truth.

Psalm 23:6 reminds us:

> **"Surely goodness and mercy shall follow me all the days of my life."**

When we dwell in God's presence, His goodness flows through us, transforming our lives and the lives of those around us.

Reflection Questions

- How has God's goodness shaped your life?

- Are there areas where you struggle to reflect true goodness?

- What practical steps can you take this week to grow in the fruit of goodness?

Closing Prayer

Lord, thank You for being the ultimate source of goodness. Teach me to reflect Your character in my actions, words, and thoughts. Help me to reject superficial goodness and embrace a life of true righteousness. Strengthen my heart to follow Your will and use me to bring Your light into the world. In Jesus' name, **Amen.**

Chapter 15

Faithfulness

Unshakable Trust

Rally Racing: Trusting the Co-Driver

In the world of rally racing, every second counts. Drivers navigate treacherous terrain at blistering speeds, cutting through sharp turns, launching over hills, and maneuvering through unpredictable weather conditions. Unlike traditional racing, where drivers memorize a set course, rally drivers depend on one thing above all—**their co-driver's voice.**

The co-driver isn't just a passenger; they are the navigator, calling out every turn, hazard, and terrain change before it even comes into sight. The driver must **trust** their instructions completely. There's no time to question, hesitate, or second-guess. If the driver delays obedience, even for a fraction of a second, they risk disaster. **Faithfulness in rally racing is full, unwavering trust—relying on the voice that guides, no matter what the road ahead looks like.**

Faithfulness: Walking in Trust with God

Faithfulness in our spiritual journey mirrors this kind of trust. The road of life is unpredictable—full of twists, unexpected obstacles, and conditions beyond our control. But we are not left to navigate it alone. **God is our navigator.** Through His Word, His Spirit, and His guidance, He gives us direction before we even see the road ahead.

> *"Trust in the LORD with all your heart and lean not on your own understanding; in all your ways submit to Him, and He will make your paths straight."* — Proverbs 3:5-6

Like a rally driver, we must commit to full trust—**not relying on our own sight but on the instructions God gives.** The driver doesn't argue with the co-driver; they listen and obey. In the same way, faithfulness to God means we trust His voice even when the path looks uncertain.

Biblical Insight: Faithfulness in Action

Faithfulness isn't just belief—it's belief **put into action.** Hebrews 11, known as the "Hall of Faith," is filled with people who trusted God completely:

Noah built an ark before the rain ever started.

Abraham left his homeland without knowing his destination.

Moses stepped into the Red Sea before it parted.

They didn't wait for perfect conditions to obey. **They followed God's voice, even when the road ahead looked impossible.**

Practical Wisdom: How to Grow in Faithfulness

Just like rally drivers **train** to build their reflexes, we must train ourselves to trust God's leading. Here's how:

Know the Navigator's Voice – Spend time in Scripture. The more familiar we are with God's Word, the easier it is to recognize His direction.

Obey Without Hesitation – Trust isn't real until it's tested. When God speaks, act without delay. Delayed obedience is disobedience.

Stay the Course – Life will bring storms, detours, and setbacks. Faithfulness means **staying committed** even when conditions change.

Real-Life Application: Faithfulness in Everyday Life

Faithfulness shows up in our lives in many ways:

In Relationships: Staying loyal and committed to our family, friends, and community, even when it's inconvenient.

In Work and Ministry: Serving with consistency and integrity, not just when it's easy.

In Trials: Holding onto God's promises, even when circumstances tempt us to doubt.

Imagine a co-driver warning about a sharp turn ahead, but the driver ignores them because the road "looks straight." Disaster is inevitable. In the same way, if we trust only what we see instead of God's voice, we will stray from the course He set for us.

Reflection Prompts

- Where is God asking you to trust Him more fully?

- Have you ever hesitated when He called you to act? What was the result?

- How can you train yourself to recognize and obey His voice more quickly?

Action Steps: Training in Faithfulness

Memorize a Key Verse – Write down **Lamentations 3:22-23**:

> *"Because of the Lord's great love we are not consumed, for His compassions never fail. They are new every morning; great is Your faithfulness."*

Read it every morning as a reminder.

Practice Instant Obedience – The next time God nudges you—whether to pray for someone, offer help, or step into a challenge—**act immediately.**

Journal a Faithfulness Log – Write down ways God has proven faithful in your life. When doubts arise, read back over His track record.

Final Encouragement: Stay in the Race

A rally driver wins not by second-guessing but by trusting every instruction. **Faithfulness is the key to finishing the race God has set before us.** If we trust Him, obey His voice, and remain steadfast no matter the road conditions, we will reach the finish line victorious.

> *"Let us hold unswervingly to the hope we profess, for He who promised is faithful."* — Hebrews 10:23

Stay the course. Trust the Navigator. Victory is ahead.

Closing Prayer

Heavenly Father,
Thank You for being faithful in every season. Help me to trust You completely, even when the road ahead looks

uncertain. Teach me to recognize Your voice and to obey without hesitation. Strengthen my faithfulness so that I may run this race with endurance, always relying on Your perfect guidance. In Jesus' name, **Amen.**

Chapter 16

Gentleness

Strength Under Control

The Art of Precision Driving

Picture a professional race car driver handling a high-powered sports car. With a tap of the accelerator, the car surges forward, capable of reaching breathtaking speeds. But raw power alone doesn't win races. **Victory comes through controlled precision—knowing when to accelerate, when to brake, and how to handle the curves without losing control.**

A reckless driver who oversteers or accelerates at the wrong moment will crash, no matter how much horsepower their car has. True mastery is not in brute force but in disciplined control.

This is the essence of **gentleness**. The world often confuses gentleness with weakness, but in reality, gentleness is **strength under control.** Just like a skilled racer harnesses the full power of their car without reckless force, a person led by the Spirit wields their strength with wisdom, patience, and care.

Jesus: The Ultimate Example of Gentleness

Gentleness is one of Jesus' defining traits. He had all power and authority, yet He approached people with compassion, humility, and grace.

To the weary and burdened, He offered rest:

> *"Take my yoke upon you and learn from me, for I am gentle and humble in heart, and you will find rest for your souls."* – Matthew 11:29

To sinners, He showed mercy instead of condemnation:
When the Pharisees wanted to stone the woman caught in adultery, Jesus responded with wisdom, disarming their accusations with a simple challenge:

"Let him who is without sin among you be the first to throw a stone at her." – John 8:7

Even in moments of confrontation, Jesus never lost control. He was firm against injustice but never aggressive or cruel. His gentleness made room for healing, transformation, and restoration.

Biblical Insight: Gentleness in Action

Gentleness is not about being passive or timid. Instead, it is the ability to **respond to others with grace, even when we have the power to do otherwise.**

Moses was described as the meekest man on earth (Numbers 12:3), yet he led Israel out of Egypt with boldness.

Paul urged believers to restore those who stumble "with a spirit of gentleness" (Galatians 6:1).

Proverbs 15:1 reminds us: *"A gentle answer turns away wrath, but a harsh word stirs up anger."*

Gentleness **protects relationships, defuses conflict, and reflects God's heart.**

Practical Wisdom: Training in Gentleness

Like a race car driver mastering their vehicle, we must train ourselves to practice gentleness:

Control Your Reactions – Before responding in frustration, take a breath. Choose patience over harshness.

Speak with Grace – Use words that encourage rather than tear down.

Lead with Compassion – Gentleness is most evident in how we treat the weak, the struggling, and those who disagree with us.

Surrender to the Holy Spirit – True gentleness isn't just human effort; it comes from allowing God to shape our character.

Real-Life Application: Where Do You Need Gentleness?

In Family: Do you respond with patience, or do you let frustration take over?

At Work/School: Do you handle conflicts with grace or

react impulsively?

On Social Media: Are your words seasoned with kindness, even when you disagree?

Gentleness isn't just a Sunday virtue—it's a way of life that transforms every interaction.

Reflection Prompts

- When was the last time you reacted in frustration instead of gentleness?

- How can you practice self-control in high-pressure situations?

- Who in your life needs a gentle response from you this week?

Action Steps: Training in Gentleness

Pause Before Responding – The next time you feel the urge to react harshly, take a deep breath and pray first.

Memorize a Key Verse – Write down **Philippians 4:5**: *"Let your gentleness be evident to all. The Lord is* *near."* Keep it in front of you as a daily reminder.

Gentleness Challenge – Choose one person you often struggle to be gentle with and make a conscious effort to respond with patience and kindness.

Final Encouragement: Strength Through Surrender

A race car is most effective when fully under the driver's control. **In the same way, our strength is most effective when surrendered to God's guidance.** Gentleness is not weakness—it is the mark of a life led by the Spirit, responding with love even when the world expects force.

> *"Blessed are the meek, for they will inherit the earth."* – Matthew 5:5

Master your strength. Choose gentleness. Reflect Jesus.

Closing Prayer

Heavenly Father,
Thank You for showing me that true strength is found

in gentleness. Help me to respond with patience and grace in every situation. Teach me to control my words, my emotions, and my actions so that I may reflect Your love. Fill me with Your Spirit, and let my gentleness be a testimony of Your power at work in me. In Jesus' name, **Amen.**

Chapter 17

Self-Control

The Finishing Stride of an Athlete of Faith

E very great race has a moment when an athlete must **push past exhaustion, ignore distractions, and unleash their final sprint.** This is what separates the good from the great—it's the test of **self-control.**

A runner who gives in to fatigue, a driver who loses focus on the track, or a competitor who gets distracted by the noise of the crowd will never reach their full potential. **Success demands discipline—mastering both body and mind to stay on course until the very end.**

As followers of Christ, our race is not just physical—it's spiritual. We must train ourselves to **resist temptation, stay focused on our purpose,**

and finish strong in the faith.

The Key to Spiritual Endurance

Self-control is not about denying ourselves joy—it's about **choosing what matters most over what we want in the moment.** It is the foundation that holds together all the other fruits of the Spirit.

Without self-control:

Love turns into indulgence.

Joy becomes recklessness.

Peace slips into complacency.

Patience fades into passivity.

Kindness weakens into people-pleasing.

Goodness twists into self-righteousness.

Faithfulness hardens into rigidity.

Gentleness dissolves into timidity.

A **life led by the Spirit requires self-control**—not as a restriction, but as the discipline that leads to true freedom.

"A person without self-control is like a city with broken-down walls." – Proverbs 25:28

In ancient times, **a city without walls was defenseless, open to attack.** In the same way, when we lack self-control, we leave ourselves open to sin, distraction, and failure. **But when we build strong walls through discipline, we protect what matters most—our faith, purpose, and integrity.**

Biblical Insight: Running the Race Well

Paul often compared the Christian life to an athlete in training:

"Everyone who competes in the games goes into strict training. They do it to get a crown that will not last, but we do it to get a crown that will last forever." – 1 Corinthians 9:25

Athletes train with purpose, discipline their bodies, and make sacrifices to achieve their goal. In the same way, **our spiritual race requires daily training, resisting distractions, and keeping our eyes on the**

ultimate prize—eternal life with Christ.

Jesus Himself practiced self-discipline:

He fasted for 40 days in the wilderness to prepare for His ministry.

He woke up early to pray, staying spiritually strong.

He endured suffering on the cross, resisting the temptation to take an easier way out.

His self-control was powered by His deep connection to the Father. And that same strength is available to us through the Holy Spirit.

The Building Blocks of Self-Discipline

Just as an athlete strengthens their body through training, we must strengthen our spirit through these key disciplines:

Mastering Your Mind – *"Renew Your Focus"*

"Do not conform to the pattern of this world, but be transformed by the renewing of your mind." – Romans 12:2

What you focus on shapes your actions.

- Fill your mind with **God's truth** instead of negativity.

- Replace distractions with **purposeful habits.**

- Train yourself to think **eternally, not just temporarily.**

Training Your Body – *"Discipline Your Actions"*

"I discipline my body and keep it under control, lest after preaching to others I myself should be disqualified." – 1 Corinthians 9:27

Self-control extends to **what we eat, how we rest, and how we use our time.**

Start small: Wake up early, limit distractions, practice fasting.

Create routines that build consistency.

Treat your body as God's temple (1 Corinthians 6:19-20).

Strengthening Your Spirit – *"Fuel Your Faith"*

> *"The spirit is willing, but the flesh is weak."* – Matthew 26:41

Spiritual discipline is like keeping your fuel tank full.

Pray daily – Seek God's strength before temptation strikes.

Read Scripture – Let God's Word shape your responses.

Surround yourself with strong believers – Community keeps you accountable.

Controlling Your Tongue – *"Power in Words"*

> *"The tongue has the power of life and death."* – Proverbs 18:21

Your words shape your world.

Speak truth, not lies.

Choose kindness over sarcasm.

Build others up instead of tearing them down.

Resisting Temptation – *"Staying on Track"*

> *"No temptation has overtaken you except what is common to mankind. And God is faithful; He will not let you be tempted beyond what you can bear." –* 1 Corinthians 10:13

Self-control is choosing **long-term victory over short-term pleasure.**

Identify your biggest weaknesses.

Set **clear boundaries** to avoid compromise.

Flee from temptation instead of flirting with it.

Real-Life Application: Where Do You Need More Discipline?

In your thoughts? (Worry, comparison, negativity?)

In your habits? (Laziness, procrastination, lack of prayer?)

In your words? (Criticism, gossip, impatience?)

In your emotions? (Anger, impatience, pride?)

Self-discipline is a **daily battle, but every small victory strengthens your faith.**

Reflection Prompts

- What is one area where you need to develop more self-control?

- What distractions are keeping you from running your race well?

- How can you start **training your spirit, mind, and body** today?

Action Steps: Training in Self-Discipline

Pick One Habit to Improve – Choose one small action to build discipline this week (e.g., wake up 10 minutes earlier for prayer).

Memorize a Key Verse – Write down **2 Timothy 1:7**:

"For the Spirit God gave us does not make

us timid, but gives us power, love, and
self-discipline."

Accountability Challenge – Tell a trusted friend your
goal and ask them to check in with you.

The "Pause Before You Act" Rule – Before making a
decision, stop and ask: **"Is this bringing me closer to
God's best for me, or pulling me away?"**

Final Encouragement: The Reward of Discipline

No athlete enjoys training in the moment, but when
the race is over, **they never regret the sacrifice.** In the
same way, self-discipline may feel hard now, but the
reward of a strong, Spirit-led life is worth it.

"Well done, good and faithful servant!" –
Matthew 25:23

**Discipline isn't about restriction—it's about
freedom. Freedom to run your race well, without
regret, and to finish strong in faith.**

Closing Prayer

*Thank You Jesus for giving me the Spirit of power, love, and self-discipline. Strengthen me to resist distractions and stay focused on the race You have set before me. Help me to train my thoughts, my habits, and my emotions so that I may reflect Your character. May my self-control bring me closer to You and inspire others to do the same. In Jesus' name, **Amen.***

Chapter 18

Love

The Finish Line

"Three things will last forever—faith, hope,
*and love—and **the greatest of these is love.**"*
— 1 Corinthians 13:13

E very athlete trains with one goal in mind—the
finish line. Championships, records, and medals
are celebrated, and for the greatest, a spot in
the **Hall of Fame** becomes the ultimate reward for
their dedication. Their legacy isn't just in their stats but
in how they endured, sacrificed, and pushed through
every obstacle to complete their race.

But in the race of faith, God's measure of success
is entirely different. He isn't counting how many
Bible verses we've memorized, how many church

services we've attended, or even how many miracles we've witnessed. Instead, He gives us one defining test: **Love.**

Love is **the finish line**. It's not an optional add-on to our faith—it's the proof that our training has been real. Every other fruit of the Spirit—joy, peace, patience, kindness, goodness, faithfulness, gentleness, and self-control—finds its root in love. Without love, everything else falls apart.

The Standard: God's Definition of Love

In **1 Corinthians 13**, we find the ultimate blueprint for what love looks like in action:

> *"If I could speak all the languages of earth and of angels, but didn't love others, I would only be a noisy gong or a clanging cymbal."* — 1 Corinthians 13:1

> *"Love is patient and kind. Love is not jealous or boastful or proud or rude. It does not demand its own way. It is not irritable, and*

it keeps no record of being wronged." — 1 Corinthians 13:4-5

We can have **great spiritual gifts, deep biblical knowledge, and even unshakable faith**—but if we don't have love, it all means nothing.

Love isn't just a feeling. It's a decision. A discipline. A lifelong training program for the soul. It requires endurance, self-sacrifice, and complete dependence on God's grace.

Why Love is the Hardest Race

Not everyone reaches **the finish line of love**.

Just like not every athlete makes it to the Hall of Fame, not every believer finishes the race of faith with love as their defining mark. Why? Because **truly loving like Jesus requires sacrifice**.

Many start strong but give up when it gets tough, thinking:

"I can't love like that. Only Jesus can."

But here's the truth: **We're not meant to love like Jesus in our own strength. We love like Him through His grace.**

Grace picks us up when we fall. It strengthens us when we're weak. It reminds us that **the race isn't over just because we stumbled**.

Loving God and loving others—beyond what they can do for us—is the true mark of those who **finish strong** in faith. This is what separates those who merely start the race from those who run to win.

A Personal Love Check

A great way to check if we're truly running toward love is to **personalize 1 Corinthians 13**. Try replacing the word *love* with your name or your role:

- *A father is patient and kind.*

- *A wife is not jealous or boastful or proud.*

- *A leader does not demand his own way.*

- *A friend never gives up, never loses faith, and endures through every circumstance.*

Does this describe us? Or does it reveal areas where we still need training?

This is our ultimate test. Not how much we know. Not how much we do. But **how much we love**.

In the end, the greatest victory won't be in what we achieved—it will be in how we loved. Because when we cross the finish line of life, the only thing that will last is **faith, hope, and love—and the greatest of these is love.**

Running the Race with Love

In any long-distance race, the real challenge isn't just starting strong—it's maintaining endurance when exhaustion sets in. The early laps feel exciting, but as the miles stretch on, fatigue, doubts, and discomfort creep in. The same is true in our race of faith.

Loving others, especially when it's inconvenient or undeserved, can feel like an uphill climb. It's easy to show kindness when we feel appreciated, but what about when we're wronged? What about when we face betrayal, rejection, or indifference?

That's why **love is the hardest race—but also the**

most rewarding. It's the test that reveals whether we're running on **human effort or God's grace**.

The Grit of Love: Pushing Past the Pain

Every elite athlete reaches a point in training where their muscles scream to stop. Their body sends signals to quit, but their mind has to push forward. This moment is called *the threshold*—the place where the body wants to break, but true strength is built.

In faith, **love has its own threshold moments**.

- When someone insults you—**will you respond with love or pride?**

- When a friend lets you down—**will you show grace or hold a grudge?**

- When loving someone means sacrificing your own comfort—**will you press on or turn away?**

Jesus gave us the ultimate example of love's endurance:

"Father, forgive them, for they don't know

what they are doing." — Luke 23:34

Even on the cross, in the most painful moment of
His life, Jesus chose love. He didn't quit. He didn't
retaliate. **He endured love's greatest test—and won.**

Love is the Mark of a True Champion

In the world of sports, champions aren't just known for
their **stats**—they're remembered for their **character**.
The greatest athletes are the ones who inspire, lift
others up, and leave a legacy beyond trophies.

In the same way, our faith will not be measured
by **how much we did**, but by **how much we loved**.

When we stand before God at the **true finish line**, He
will ask:

"Did you learn to love like My Son?"

This is the real victory. This is the gold medal of
faith. **Because in the end, only love will remain.**

Love: The Training Plan

If love is the race that matters most, then we need a training plan. Just like an athlete disciplines their body, **we must discipline our hearts to love like Jesus**.

Here's a simple **daily workout** for growing in love:

Warm-Up: Start with God's Love

Before we can love others, we must first receive God's love. Begin each day by reminding yourself:
"I am fully loved by God—not because of what I do, but because of who He is."

> *"We love each other because He loved us first."* — 1 John 4:19

Strength Training: Love in Action

Every day brings opportunities to train in love. **Look for one way** to show kindness, patience, or forgiveness—especially when it's difficult.

"Don't just pretend to love others. Really love them." — Romans 12:9

Endurance Building: Press Through the Hard Days

Some days, love feels easy. Other days, it feels impossible. **This is where endurance is built.** On the hardest days, lean on grace and refuse to quit.

"Love never gives up, never loses faith, is always hopeful, and endures through every circumstance." — 1 Corinthians 13:7

Cool-Down: Reflection & Prayer

End each day by reflecting:

- Did I love well today?

- Where did I fall short?

- How can I grow tomorrow?

Ask God to fill you with His love so you can keep running strong.

"May the Lord make your love for one another and for all people grow and overflow." — 1 Thessalonians 3:12

Real-Life Application: Love in the Everyday Race

Love isn't just for big, dramatic moments—it's built in the small, everyday choices we make. Just like an athlete's strength is developed through consistent training, our love for others grows through daily practice.

At home, love is tested when relationships grow tense. When your sibling, spouse, or parent frustrates you, do you react in anger, or respond in patience? Are you quick to forgive, or do you hold onto past mistakes? These moments are like intervals in an athlete's training—they help you build endurance in love.

At work or school, love is demonstrated through acts of service and kindness. Do you show kindness to those who are difficult or ignored? Are you willing to help others, even when it's inconvenient? The decisions you make in these settings shape your faith and reflect the love of Christ to those around you.

In public, love is challenged in how we treat strangers. Do you treat others with respect, even when you're in a rush? How do you respond when someone cuts you off in traffic or takes the last item on the shelf? These are the moments that test our character, where our love can shine the brightest or falter the most.

On social media, love is evident in our words. Do your words build others up, or do they tear down? Are you more focused on proving a point, or showing Christ-like love? In today's world, the way we interact online is just as important as how we act in person.

Jesus said:

> *"Your love for one another will prove to the world that you are my disciples"* — John 13:35

Love is the evidence of our faith. The world isn't watching how much we pray or how many Bible verses we know—they are watching how we love.

Reflection Prompts: Measuring Your Love Endurance

Check Your Course: Take a moment to reflect. How do you respond when love requires patience or sacrifice? When was the last time you showed love to someone who didn't deserve it?

Evaluate Your Race: Love is not a sprint but a marathon. Do you love others only when it's easy, or do you push through when it's hard? Where in your life are you struggling to love like Jesus?

Set a Love Goal: Reflect on where you need to grow. What is one area in your life where you need to grow in love? Who in your life do you need to love better this week?

Action Steps: Training in Love

Meditate on Love Daily: Each morning this week, read 1 Corinthians 13. Replace the word "love" with your name (e.g., "John is patient and kind"). Let this passage sink into your heart and guide your actions.

Choose One Love Challenge: Identify one person

who is difficult to love and commit to praying for them daily. Take action by performing an act of kindness for someone without expecting anything in return.

Apologize & Reconcile: If there is someone you need to forgive or ask forgiveness from, take the first step today. Love involves humility, and reconciliation is a powerful expression of that love.

Pray for More Love: Ask God to fill you with His love so that you can love others better. Don't rely on your own strength—His grace is what empowers us to love beyond our natural abilities.

Closing Prayer: A Champion's Prayer for Love

Heavenly Father,

You are the source of true love. I know that without You, my love is weak and imperfect. But through Your grace, I can love like Jesus. Help me to grow in patience, kindness, and forgiveness. When love feels difficult, strengthen me. When I fall short, remind me of Your grace.

Lord, I want to finish this race well. Teach me to love

boldly, selflessly, and sacrificially. Let my life reflect Your love so that others may see You in me.

*In Jesus' name, **Amen.***

Chapter 19

Elite's Training

An elite athlete doesn't just train for a single event; they train for a lifetime of competition. They don't develop strength in only one area of their body but strive for complete fitness—stamina, agility, endurance, and discipline. In the same way, an Athlete of Faith cannot rely on one virtue alone. The fruits of the Spirit are not optional accessories; they are essential components of a well-trained spiritual life.

When we look back at the nine fruits—Love, Joy, Peace, Patience, Kindness, Goodness, Faithfulness, Gentleness, and Self-Control—we see a divine training plan laid out before us. These are not merely qualities to admire; they are strengths to cultivate. Just as a runner must stretch, a weightlifter must build resistance, and a boxer must learn precision, we, too, must train in these virtues daily.

The Fruits in Action

Imagine a Christian who is strong in faith but lacks love—would they be able to represent Christ well? What about a believer who knows Scripture but lacks patience—how would they guide others with wisdom? Each fruit strengthens a different part of our spiritual muscle, and together, they make us complete.

Love teaches us to train with the right motivation.

Joy sustains us through hardships.

Peace anchors us in life's storms.

Patience equips us for endurance.

Kindness makes us approachable and compassionate.

Goodness ensures our integrity.

Faithfulness keeps us committed.

Gentleness helps us correct and lead with humility.

Self-control guards us from self-sabotage.

To be an Athlete of Faith is to recognize that spiritual training is not a one-time event. Just like an athlete

adjusts their workouts based on their weaknesses,
we must assess our spiritual growth. Which fruits
are flourishing in your life? Which ones need more
training?

The Call to Continue Training

In Philippians 3:14, Paul reminds us:

> *"I press on toward the goal to win the prize
> for which God has called me heavenward in
> Christ Jesus."*

No matter how much we grow, there will always be
another challenge ahead. The enemy will attempt to
test our patience, shake our peace, or lure us away
from goodness. But when we train with the Spirit,
we are not alone. We are under the guidance of the
greatest Coach—God Himself.

As we conclude this chapter, remember that the goal
is not perfection but progress. If you fall, get back up.
If a particular fruit is difficult to cultivate, ask the Holy
Spirit for help. Just like an athlete who wakes up early
for training, we must be willing to show up daily for our

faith.

Reflection Prompts:

1. Which fruit of the Spirit do you feel strongest in? Which one do you need to train more?

2. How have you seen these fruits impact your relationships?

3. What challenges have tested your patience, peace, or love recently? How did you respond?

4. In what ways can you intentionally cultivate these fruits this week?

Action Steps:

Select one fruit to focus on strengthening this week.

Find a Scripture related to that fruit and meditate on it daily.

Pray each morning, asking the Holy Spirit to help you grow in this area.

At the end of the week, reflect on any growth or challenges you encountered.

Closing Prayer:

*Heavenly Father, thank You for the gift of Your Spirit that produces these fruits in our lives. I ask for Your strength to train in love, joy, peace, patience, kindness, goodness, faithfulness, gentleness, and self-control. Where I am weak, Lord, strengthen me. Help me to reflect Christ in my words, actions, and thoughts. May I run this race with endurance, trusting that You are refining me daily. In Jesus' name, A***men.**

With this foundation, we are now prepared for the next phase of training. It's time to learn how to overcome the obstacles that threaten to slow us down. Let's move forward to the next chapter: Recognizing the Enemy's Traps.

Recognizing the Enemy's Traps

Overcoming Obstacles

A runner doesn't just train for endurance; they prepare for obstacles. A hurdler knows that every race will have barriers. A boxer anticipates their opponent's punches. A soldier is trained to identify traps before they step into danger. In the same way, an Athlete of Faith must be aware that the journey of faith isn't just about growing stronger—it's also about recognizing and overcoming the traps that the enemy sets to hinder us.

When we commit to living as a Jesus Man or Jesus Woman, we must understand that we are stepping into a spiritual battleground. The enemy will try to distract us, weaken us, and pull us off course. Many believers fall, not because they lack passion, but because they are unaware of these spiritual attacks.

In the following chapters, we will examine some of the most common spiritual obstacles, their impact, and how we can overcome them with God's strength.

Chapter 20

Fear

The Opponent of Faith

F ear is a thief. It steals confidence, joy, and progress. It is a spiritual trap designed to keep believers from stepping into the fullness of what God has called them to do. Fear whispers lies: *"You're not good enough." "God won't come through for you." "What if you fail?"* But faith shouts back, *"God is with me." "His promises never fail." "I am more than a conqueror through Christ."*

As we pursue a life of spiritual growth—one where we supplement our faith with moral excellence, knowledge, self-control, and endurance (2 Peter 1:5-7)—we must first recognize that fear is an enemy of that growth. It keeps us from moving forward, from trusting God's voice, and from living in the boldness we were meant to have as Jesus Men and Jesus

Women.

The Nature of Fear

At its core, fear is not just an emotion; it is a spiritual force. In the natural world, fear can serve a purpose—it alerts us to danger and helps us react in emergencies. But in the spiritual realm, fear is a tool the enemy uses to paralyze believers. It distorts our perception of reality, making mountains out of molehills and causing us to see obstacles as insurmountable.

Fear is also deceptive. It often masquerades as wisdom. How many times have we hesitated to obey God, thinking we were just being "cautious" when, in reality, we were afraid? The Bible is clear that fear does not come from God.

> *"For God has not given us a spirit of*
> *fear and timidity, but of power, love, and*
> *self-discipline."* – 2 Timothy 1:7

If fear does not come from God, then it is something we must learn to reject. Just as an athlete learns to reject laziness and distractions, we must reject fear when it tries to creep into our minds and hearts.

How Fear Manifests in Our Lives

Fear of Failure

The thought: *"What if I step out in faith and I fail?"*

The truth: Failure is not final. The greatest men and women of faith experienced failure before their victories. Peter denied Jesus, yet became the rock on which the church was built. Moses doubted his ability to speak, yet led a nation to freedom. God doesn't ask for perfection—He asks us to not give up. To endure in faith.

Fear of Rejection

The thought: *"What if people don't accept me? What if they judge me for my faith?"*

The truth: Jesus was rejected by many, yet He remained obedient to His mission. If we live for people's approval, we will always be controlled by their opinions. True freedom comes when we live for God's approval.

Fear of the Unknown

The thought: *"What if I follow God, and things don't turn out the way I hoped?"*

The truth: Faith is about trusting God even when we can't see the whole picture. Abraham didn't know where he was going when God told him to leave his homeland, but he trusted. Walking by faith means stepping forward even when we don't have all the answers.

Fear of Lack

The thought: *"What if I don't have enough? Enough money, enough resources, enough strength?"*

The truth: God is our provider. Jesus reminds us in Matthew 6:26 that if God cares for the birds of the air, He will certainly care for us. Fear of lack makes us hold on tightly to things we should release. Faith allows us to trust that God will provide.

Overcoming Fear with the Truth of God's Word

The only way to conquer fear is through faith. And

faith comes by hearing and believing God's Word (Romans 10:17). Here are some powerful promises to counteract fear:

When you fear failure: **"I can do all things through Christ who strengthens me."** – Philippians 4:13

When you fear rejection: **"If God is for us, who can be against us?"** – Romans 8:31

When you fear the unknown: **"Trust in the Lord with all your heart and lean not on your own understanding."** – Proverbs 3:5

When you fear lack: **"My God will supply all your needs according to His riches in glory in Christ Jesus."** – Philippians 4:19

The Faith of a Spiritual Athlete

An athlete faces fears every time they step onto the field or court. They fear losing, making mistakes, or disappointing their coach. But they don't let those fears stop them—they push forward. They trust their training, they listen to their coach's voice, and they take bold action.

As believers, we must train ourselves to do the same.

We silence fear by trusting in God's training, listening to the Holy Spirit, and taking bold steps of faith.

Reflection Prompts

- In what areas of your life has fear been holding you back?

- How can you apply God's promises to silence fear in your heart?

- What step of faith do you need to take today to overcome fear?

Action Steps

Write It Down: Identify one fear that has been limiting you and write a Bible verse next to it that speaks against it.

Pray with Boldness: Ask God to replace fear with faith and declare His promises over your life.

Take a Step of Faith: Do something that fear has been stopping you from doing—whether it's sharing your testimony, stepping into a leadership role, or making a decision in obedience to God.

Closing Prayer

Father, I thank You that You have not given me a spirit of fear, but of power, love, and a sound mind. Today, I choose to reject fear and walk in faith. Help me to trust You completely, even when I don't see the whole picture. Give me the courage to take bold steps, knowing that You are always with me. In Jesus' name, **Amen.**

Chapter 21

Pride

The Silent Killer

P ride is one of the most dangerous spiritual
traps because it is deceptive. Unlike fear, which
often feels uncomfortable and restrictive, pride can
feel empowering. It whispers, *"You don't need help."*
*"You're doing just fine on your own." "You're better than
others."* But while pride may appear strong on the
surface, it is actually a weakness that keeps us from
fully depending on God.

The Bible warns us clearly:

> *"Pride goes before destruction, and
> haughtiness before a fall."* – Proverbs 16:18
> (NLT)

Pride sets us on a path toward spiritual downfall. It

blinds us to our weaknesses, makes us resistant to correction, and distances us from God's guidance. If we are to train as spiritual athletes, we must recognize and defeat pride before it defeats us.

The Nature of Pride

At its core, pride is a form of self-reliance. It tells us that we don't need God's help, that we can rely on our own strength and wisdom. While confidence is a good thing, there is a fine line between confidence and arrogance. True confidence comes from knowing who we are in Christ. Pride, on the other hand, places our trust in ourselves rather than in God.

The first sin in the Bible was not disobedience—it was pride. Lucifer, once a high-ranking angel, was cast out of heaven because he wanted to elevate himself above God (Isaiah 14:12-15). Pride led to his downfall, and it has been a primary tool of the enemy ever since.

How Pride Manifests in Our Lives

Self-Sufficiency

The thought: *"I don't need anyone's help. I can do this* *on my own."*

The truth: God created us to live in dependence on Him and in community with others. Even Jesus, who was fully God, depended on the Father in prayer (John 5:19).

Resistance to Correction

The thought: *"I don't need to change. I already know what I'm doing."*

The truth: Wise people accept correction and grow from it. Proverbs 12:1 says, **"To learn, you must love discipline; it is stupid to hate correction."**

Comparison and Superiority

The thought: *"At least I'm better than that person."*

The truth: God calls us to humility. Romans 12:3 warns us **"not to think you are better than you really are."** Pride leads us to judge others instead of focusing on our own growth.

False Humility

The thought: *"I'm just a humble servant" (but secretly* *wanting recognition).*

The truth: True humility doesn't seek approval. It serves because of love, not because of a need for validation (Matthew 6:1-4).

Overcoming Pride with Humility

If pride is the disease, humility is the cure. But humility is not thinking less of yourself—it is thinking of yourself less. It is recognizing that all good things come from God, and that without Him, we can do nothing (John 15:5).

Here are some ways to cultivate humility:

Acknowledge Your Dependence on God. Instead of relying on your own strength, make it a habit to pray, seek God's wisdom, and trust in His plan.

Be Open to Correction. Ask God to give you a teachable heart. Surround yourself with wise, godly people who can speak truth into your life.

Serve Others Without Seeking Recognition. Jesus washed His disciples' feet, an act of humility and love (John 13:12-17). Look for ways to serve without expecting praise.

Regularly Examine Your Heart. Ask yourself: *"Am I doing this for God's glory or for my own?"* Invite the Holy Spirit to reveal any prideful areas in your life.

Reflection Prompts

- In what areas of your life have you been relying on your own strength instead of God's?

- How do you respond when someone corrects you?

- What are some practical ways you can serve others with humility this week?

Closing Prayer

"Father, I recognize that pride is a subtle enemy that can creep into my heart unnoticed. I ask for Your help in keeping me humble. Teach me to rely on You rather than my own strength. Give me a heart that is teachable, a spirit that is willing to serve, and a mind that seeks to glorify You above all else. In Jesus' name, Amen."

Chapter 22

Anger

The Uncontrolled Fire

Anger, when left unchecked, is like an uncontrolled fire—it consumes everything in its path. It damages relationships, clouds our judgment, and distances us from God. While anger itself is not a sin, how we handle it determines whether it becomes a spiritual trap or a tool for growth.

The Bible offers a clear warning:

> **"Human anger does not produce the righteousness God desires."** – James 1:20 (NLT)

This verse reminds us that anger, when driven by the flesh, rarely leads to good outcomes. However, anger can be harnessed for a righteous purpose when controlled by the Holy Spirit. The key is learning to recognize the difference.

Understanding Anger: Righteous vs. Sinful

Not all anger is sinful. Jesus Himself displayed righteous anger when He cleansed the temple, overturning the tables of money changers who had turned God's house into a marketplace (Matthew 21:12-13). This kind of anger was fueled by a passion for God's holiness and justice.

But sinful anger is different. It is rooted in pride, selfishness, or an unwillingness to forgive. It leads to bitterness, resentment, and division. The Bible cautions:

"Don't sin by letting anger control you. Don't let the sun go down while you are still angry, for anger gives a foothold to the devil." – Ephesians 4:26-27 (NLT)

If anger is not dealt with quickly and properly, it becomes a tool for the enemy to create division, hurt, and destruction in our lives.

How Anger Manifests in Our Lives

Explosive Rage

The thought: *"I just lost control."*

The truth: Losing control is a choice. Proverbs 29:11 says, **"Fools vent their anger, but the wise quietly hold it back."**

Silent Resentment

The thought: *"I'm fine." (But inside, bitterness is growing.)*

The truth: Bottling up anger is just as dangerous as exploding in rage. Hebrews 12:15 warns that bitterness **"corrupts many."**

Holding Grudges

The thought: *"I'll never forgive them."*

The truth: Jesus calls us to forgive, just as He has forgiven us (Colossians 3:13). Unforgiveness only enslaves us.

Passive-Aggressiveness

The thought: *"I won't say anything, but I'll make them regret it."*

The truth: Manipulating others through subtle anger is still sinful. Ephesians 4:31 urges us to **"get rid of all bitterness, rage, anger, and harsh words."**

Overcoming Anger with Self-Control and Love

Since anger itself is not inherently sinful, we must learn how to handle it in a way that aligns with God's righteousness. Here are some biblical strategies to gain victory over anger:

Pause Before Reacting. James 1:19 advises, **"Be quick to listen, slow to speak, and slow to get angry."** Taking a moment to pause and pray before responding prevents regretful words and actions.

Identify the Root Cause. Anger is often a symptom of deeper issues like fear, pride, or unmet expectations. Ask God to reveal the true source.

Turn Anger into Prayer. Instead of letting anger fester, bring it to God. The Psalms are full of examples where David poured out his frustrations before the Lord.

Practice Forgiveness. Jesus commands us to forgive, even when it's difficult. Holding onto anger only poisons our own hearts.

Seek Reconciliation, Not Revenge. Romans 12:18 reminds us, **"Do all that you can to live in peace with everyone."** Humility and grace should always guide our actions.

Reflection Prompts

1. What situations or people trigger anger in your life?

2. Do you tend to explode in anger, or suppress it?

3. How can you turn moments of anger into opportunities for spiritual growth?

Closing Prayer

"Father, I recognize that anger can be a destructive force in my life if I allow it to control me. Teach me how to handle anger in a way that honors You. Help me to

pause before reacting, to forgive quickly, and to seek peace rather than revenge. Fill me with Your patience and love, so that my words and actions reflect Your grace. In Jesus' name, Amen."

Chapter 23

Distraction
The Silent Thief

Distraction is one of the enemy's most subtle and effective traps. Unlike fear or anger, which are obvious in their effects, distraction quietly steals our time, attention, and spiritual focus without us realizing it. It doesn't always come in the form of sinful temptations—sometimes, it's simply too many good things pulling us away from the best thing: intimacy with God.

Jesus warns us about this in the Parable of the Sower:

"The seed that fell among the thorns represents others who hear God's word, but all too quickly the message is crowded out by the worries of this life, the lure of wealth, and the desire for other things, so no fruit is produced." – Mark 4:18-19 (NLT)

Distraction is a thief that robs us of spiritual growth. It keeps us busy but ineffective, constantly moving but never advancing.

The Many Forms of Distraction

Technology & Entertainment can consume hours of our time before we even realize it. Social media, endless scrolling, binge-watching, and gaming often take priority over deepening our relationship with God. Instead of filling our hearts with His presence, we fill our minds with noise, leaving little room for His voice.

Busyness & Overcommitment may seem productive, but even good things can become distractions when they leave us with no time for prayer and reflection. Work, social events, and even ministry can keep us occupied but spiritually dry. We might be doing a lot, but failing to be with God.

Worry & Anxiety keep us mentally distracted, constantly thinking about the future, our problems, or our plans instead of trusting God in the present. Jesus reminds us, *"Seek first the kingdom of God… and all these things will be given to you."* – Matthew 6:33

Materialism & Success can shift our focus away from God. Chasing wealth, promotions, or status can seem like progress, but if we're not careful, we become like Martha—so busy working that we miss the presence of Jesus (Luke 10:38-42).

Recognizing When Distraction is Winning

Ask yourself: Do I find it hard to focus when I pray or read the Bible? Do I feel like I have no time for God? Do I spend more time on entertainment and social media than on spiritual growth? Am I constantly busy but spiritually drained?

If you answered "yes" to any of these, distraction might be robbing you of deeper intimacy with God.

Overcoming Distraction & Restoring Focus

Prioritize Time with God by setting a dedicated time each day for prayer and Scripture. Treat it as a non-negotiable appointment. Jesus often withdrew to quiet places to pray (Luke 5:16). If He needed this, how much more do we?

Create Boundaries for Technology by limiting social

media, setting time limits on apps, or designating "phone-free" hours. Psalm 46:10 reminds us: *"Be still, and know that I am God."*

Learn to Say No because not every opportunity is from God. Busyness isn't always a sign of fruitfulness. Ask yourself, *"Does this bring me closer to God, or is it just another distraction?"*

Replace Distractions with Devotion by transforming wasted time into worship time. Instead of mindless scrolling, listen to worship music, a sermon, or an audiobook that strengthens your faith.

Reflection Prompts

Where do distractions show up most in your life? How can you create more space for God in your daily routine? What practical steps will you take this week to remove distractions?

Action Steps

Schedule a distraction-free time with God every day—even if it's just 10 minutes to start. Fast from one major distraction (social media, TV, unnecessary busyness) for a week and replace that time with prayer. Memorize Mark 4:18-19 as a reminder to guard against distractions.

Closing Prayer

Father, I confess that I often allow distractions to take my focus away from You. I don't want to be like the seed among the thorns, losing my fruitfulness because of the worries and distractions of this world. Teach me to guard my time and attention so that I can seek You first. Help me to remove anything that keeps me from growing in You. In Jesus' name, **Amen.**

Chapter 24

Building Spiritual Endurance

"Let us run with endurance the race God has set before us." – Hebrews 12:1

Endurance separates casual players from elite athletes. In any sport, it's not just about skill or talent—it's about the ability to keep going when the race is long, the body is tired, and obstacles stand in the way. The same is true for our spiritual journey. Many Christians start strong but struggle to stay faithful when faced with trials, distractions, or discouragement.

Building spiritual endurance means learning to persevere through difficulties while keeping our eyes on Christ. It's about moving beyond short bursts of passion and developing a deep, unwavering faith that lasts a lifetime.

Why Endurance Matters in Our Faith

The Bible repeatedly emphasizes the importance of perseverance.

James 1:12 declares:

> *"Blessed is the one who perseveres under trial because, having stood the test, that person will receive the crown of life that the Lord has promised to those who love him."*

Galatians 6:9 encourages us:

> *"Let us not become weary in doing good, for at the proper time we will reap a harvest if we do not give up."*

And Romans 5:3-4 reminds us that:

> *"suffering produces perseverance;*

perseverance, character; and character, hope."

Endurance is what allows us to finish the race and receive the reward God has promised. Without it, we may start strong but never reach the finish line.

The Challenges to Spiritual Endurance

Just as runners face exhaustion, pain, and mental battles, believers also face obstacles that threaten to slow them down or make them quit.

Spiritual Fatigue can leave us feeling empty, as if our prayers go unanswered and our efforts seem fruitless. The solution is to renew our strength in God.

> *"For I can do everything through Christ, who gives me strength."* — Philippian 4:13

Delays & Waiting on God test our patience when we expect immediate results but God works through seasons of waiting. Trusting God's timing is key. Joseph endured years in prison before his promotion. David waited before becoming king. God's plans unfold perfectly, even when we can't see it.

Trials & Suffering can discourage us through illness, financial struggles, or relationship problems. However, James 1:2 teaches us to *"consider it pure joy"* when we face trials, knowing they strengthen our faith.

Discouragement & Doubt creep in when progress is slow or prayers seem unanswered. The way to combat this is by standing on God's promises. When Jesus was tempted in the wilderness, He responded with Scripture. We must do the same, using God's Word as our foundation.

Strengthening Your Spiritual Endurance

Keep Your Eyes on Jesus because Hebrews 12:2 reminds us to *"fix our eyes on Jesus, the pioneer and perfecter of faith."* Runners who focus on the pain slow down, but those who focus on the finish line push through.

Develop a Daily Discipline by training your spirit just as athletes train their bodies. Prayer and Bible study are essential, while fasting and worship deepen our dependence on God.

Surround Yourself with Encouragers who will help you persevere. Ecclesiastes 4:9-10 says, *"Two are better than one… If either of them falls down, one can help the other up."* Running alone is hard, but having a strong faith community makes the journey easier.

Trust God's Training Plan because He is your ultimate coach, shaping you for greater things. Proverbs 3:5-6 urges us to *"trust in the Lord with all your heart."* Challenges don't come to break us but to strengthen us for the race ahead.

Reflection Prompts

- **Have you ever felt like giving up spiritually?** Think about what helped you keep going.

- **What distractions or struggles are making your faith journey harder?** Identify them so you can address them.

- **How can you strengthen your endurance starting this week?** Consider what steps you can take to grow stronger in faith.

Action Steps

Memorize Hebrews 12:1-2 as a reminder to run your race with perseverance.
Commit to a spiritual discipline such as daily prayer, fasting, or Bible reading to strengthen your faith.
Find an accountability partner—someone who can encourage and pray for you as you grow in endurance.

Closing Prayer

*Lord, I confess that sometimes I grow weary in my faith. Help me to run this race with endurance, trusting You even when the journey is tough. Strengthen me in trials, encourage me when I feel weak, and keep my eyes fixed on You. I know that You are preparing a great reward for those who endure. In Jesus' name, **Amen.***

Chapter 25

The Power of Correction

Faith Refinenment

Roger Federer, one of the greatest tennis players of all time, wasn't always the composed and graceful champion we admire. In his early years, he was known for his fiery temper—he would smash rackets, argue with referees, and allow his frustration to dictate his game. His talent was undeniable, but without discipline, it was incomplete.

Everything changed when Federer embraced correction. He realized that raw talent alone wouldn't make him a champion—he needed refinement. His coach became his mirror, pointing out weaknesses, not to discourage him, but to mold him into the best version of himself. Federer learned to control his emotions, sharpen his footwork, and master his precision. He became a legend, not because he resisted correction, but because he welcomed it.

This principle extends far beyond sports. Whether in our marriages, parenting, workplaces, or churches, the ability to accept and offer correction with humility and wisdom is essential. Just as Federer sought correction to improve his game, we must seek godly counsel to refine our character.

> *"Whoever loves discipline loves knowledge, but whoever hates correction is stupid."* – Proverbs 12:1

The Athlete's Perspective on Correction

In a sailing competition, adjusting the sail based on shifting winds can unleash sudden bursts of speed, allowing a competitor to overcome opposition. The same applies in faith—small course corrections, when made in obedience to God, can propel us forward in ways we never imagined.

Athletes don't view correction as an insult; they see it as the key to victory. That's why they invest in coaches who analyze every movement, looking for hidden improvements. The greatest competitors don't just accept correction—they *pay* for it. Why? Because they know that unseen weaknesses, if left unchecked, will hold them back.

Spiritually, we must adopt the same mindset. God corrects us, not to punish, but to refine. His discipline brings to the surface what needs to be strengthened, shaping us into His image.

> *"For the Lord disciplines the one He loves, and chastises every son whom He receives."* – Hebrews 12:6

Correction: The Mark of Spiritual Maturity

Correction is not a sign of failure—it is a stepping stone to greatness. An athlete who ignores feedback will never reach their full potential, and a believer who resists God's correction will never grow into the person He has called them to be.

Nathan and David (2 Samuel 12): When David sinned, Nathan confronted him with a parable that opened his eyes. Instead of resisting, David repented, leading to his restoration.

Jesus and Peter (Matthew 16:23): When Peter tried to stop Jesus from fulfilling His mission, Jesus corrected him firmly but with love. This correction ultimately prepared Peter to lead the early church.

Both examples show that correction, when embraced, leads to transformation and purpose.

How to Receive Correction with a Teachable Spirit

Great athletes don't just tolerate correction—they crave it. Spiritually, we must develop the same hunger.

See Correction as an Act of Love

> *"Wounds from a friend can be trusted, but an enemy multiplies kisses."* – Proverbs 27:6

A true friend corrects out of love, while an enemy flatters to keep us blind to our faults.

Choose Words Wisely When Giving Correction

"Let your conversation be always full of grace, seasoned with salt." – Colossians 4:6

Gentle words open hearts, while harsh words create walls. Correction should build, not break.

Check Your Own Heart Before Correcting Others

Jesus warns in Matthew 7:3-5 to remove the plank from our own eye before pointing out the speck in someone else's. A humble heart makes correction fruitful.

The Impact of Correction in Relationships

In Parenting: Children thrive when correction is balanced with love. *"Do not exasperate your children; instead, bring them up in the training and instruction of the Lord."* (Ephesians 6:4)

In Marriage: Correction should strengthen, not criticize. *"Two are better than one... if either of them* *falls, one can help the other up."* (Ecclesiastes 4:9-10)

In Church and Work: Unity flourishes when correction is done in love. *"If someone is caught in a sin, you who live by the Spirit should restore that person gently."* (Galatians 6:1)

Training to Embrace Correction

Correction is an essential part of spiritual maturity. It transforms mistakes into lessons, obstacles into stepping stones, and faith into something unshakable. If we obey God's correction and His Word, we will bear abundant fruit.

> *"He who began a good work in you will carry it on to completion until the day of Christ Jesus."* – Philippians 1:6

Reflection Prompts

- When was a time correction helped you grow spiritually or personally?

- How do you typically respond to correction?

With humility or resistance?

- Who in your life do you trust to give godly correction?

Action Steps

Pray for a teachable spirit that welcomes correction.

Identify one area where God is refining you and lean into His correction.

Thank someone who has corrected you in love and helped you grow.

Closing Prayer

*Heavenly Father, thank You for loving me enough to correct me. Help me to see Your discipline as a gift and not a burden. Give me humility to receive correction and wisdom to offer it with grace. Refine me like gold, shaping me into who You've called me to be. In Jesus' name, **Amen.***

Chapter 26

Finishing Strong

The Race of a Lifetime

E very athlete knows that the greatest test isn't in the first sprint, the early victories, or the easy training days. **The real test comes in the final stretch**—when muscles burn, lungs scream for air, and the body begs to stop. This is the moment that separates those who finish from those who falter. It is in this moment that a champion is made.

Faith is no different.

The abundant life Jesus promised is not a life without hardship, but a life where **every challenge becomes a stepping stone toward greatness.** It is the relentless pursuit of something higher, greater, and eternal. It is training the spirit to press on, even when every obstacle tries to hold you back.

In the journey of faith, **resistance is part of growth.** The sprinter builds speed by pushing against the ground. The weightlifter gains strength by battling gravity. The boxer sharpens his reflexes by taking hits and learning to recover faster. **The struggle is not a sign of weakness—it is the very thing that makes us stronger.**

We do not run aimlessly. We do not train in vain. Every discipline, every sacrifice, every moment of perseverance is for a crown that will never fade. Athletes chase trophies that rust, records that are broken, and titles that are forgotten. But those who run the race of faith with endurance are chasing a **glory that lasts forever.**

The abundant life is not about having more—it is about becoming more. It is not about avoiding losses—it is about learning from them. The best teams don't quit after a bad season; they review their mistakes, train harder, and come back stronger. The best competitors don't focus on their failures; they focus on the next opportunity to rise. **Every setback is a setup for a greater victory.**

In the moments of exhaustion, when faith feels

stretched thin, when prayers seem unanswered, and when trials press in from every side, that is where **grit is built.** That is where we choose whether to give in to the flesh or stand firm in the Spirit. That is where we realize that God is not just a spectator in our race—**He is our coach, our strength, and our source of endurance.**

He doesn't just want us to start well—**He wants us to finish strong.**

An athlete does not win by relying on past training alone. Every day requires renewed discipline, fresh focus, and the determination to push beyond yesterday's limits. In the same way, faith is not a one-time decision but a lifelong commitment to keep growing, keep learning, and keep trusting.

God does not call us to a life of comfort; He calls us to a life of transformation. And transformation requires challenge. The champions of faith—the ones who stand at the finish line with victory in their hands—are those who have endured every trial with unwavering trust, knowing that **God wastes nothing.**

No pain, no loss, no failure is without purpose. Every moment in this race is shaping us, refining us, and preparing us for the eternal reward that awaits. We don't just run for today—we run for eternity.

So as you step forward, remember this: The race is long, but the reward is worth it. **Keep your eyes on the prize. Keep training. Keep growing. Keep running with endurance.** And when your race is done, may you stand before God, not just as someone who believed—but as someone who **gave everything** for the Kingdom.

Finish strong. The crown is waiting.

Prayer for Finishing Strong

Heavenly Father,

You are the author of my race, the strength in my weakness, and the coach who never leaves my side. You have called me to run with endurance, to press forward when I feel weary, and to trust in You when the road ahead seems uncertain.

Lord, train my heart to seek You above all else. When challenges arise, let me not shrink back in fear, but rise up in faith. When I stumble, remind me that Your grace is greater than my failures. When I feel like giving up, breathe new life into my spirit and help me press on toward the prize You have set before me.

Teach me to see every obstacle as an opportunity, every trial as a test of endurance, and every setback as a step closer to the victory You have prepared for me. Shape me into an athlete of faith—disciplined, steadfast, and unshaken by the storms of life. Let my perseverance bring You glory, and may my journey inspire others to run after You with all their heart.

I declare that my race will not be run in vain. I will not be distracted by what is temporary, but I will fix my eyes on what is eternal. I will run with purpose, with passion, and with a heart fully surrendered to Your will. And on the day I cross the finish line, may I hear Your voice say, **"Well done, good and faithful servant."**

In Jesus' mighty name,
Amen.

Chapter 27

Your End... His New Begining in You

"But those who trust in the Lord will find new strength. They will soar high on wings like eagles. They will run and not grow weary. They will walk and not faint."
— Isaiah 40:31

Your journey of faith does not end with the final words of this book. In fact, this is just the starting line. Just like an athlete who doesn't stop training after one victory, we are called to keep growing, keep pressing forward, and keep running our race with endurance.

My prayer is that this book has given you a

fresh perspective—a guide to strengthen your faith, overcome obstacles, and live a Spirit-led life. But now, the real challenge begins: applying what you have learned.

Your Faith Needs Ongoing Training

Faith is not a single moment of decision; it's a lifelong pursuit of growth. Just as an athlete builds strength through daily training, our faith is strengthened through constant practice. 2 Peter 1:3-9 urges us to add excellence, knowledge, self-control, endurance, godliness, and love to our faith. If we neglect these, we risk becoming stagnant.

The best athletes don't train only when they feel like it. They push through fatigue, distractions, and setbacks because they know that discipline leads to victory. In the same way, your spiritual endurance is built in the moments when you choose to trust God, even when life gets hard.

Commit to these habits as you continue your race:

- **Stay rooted in Scripture** – Daily time in God's Word is your fuel.

- **Prioritize prayer** – Talk to God and listen for His voice.

- **Walk in the Spirit** – Let the Holy Spirit guide your decisions.

- **Be Planted in Church** – Don't just attend—belong, serve, and learn to lead in love and spirit.

- **Stay in community** – Surround yourself with believers who push you to grow.

- **Serve others** – Live out your faith through love and generosity.

When You Fall, Get Back Up

Every athlete stumbles. They miss a shot, lose a match, or fall behind in a race. But what separates the best from the rest is their ability to get back up, shake off the failure, and press forward.

The same is true for your walk with Christ. There will be moments when you fall short, when doubt creeps in, when you feel weak. But remember: failure is not final. Proverbs 24:16 reminds us:

"The godly may trip seven times, but they will get up again."

Don't let a single failure define your story. Confess, learn, and keep going. The key to spiritual endurance is not perfection—it's perseverance.

A Final Challenge: Become a Spiritual Athlete for Others

The ultimate goal of this journey isn't just personal growth; it's transformation that impacts the world around you. Athletes don't just train for themselves—they inspire, coach, and uplift others.

- **Be an encourager** – Speak life into those who are struggling.

- **Be a mentor** – Walk alongside younger believers and help them grow.

- **Be a light** – Let your faith shine in your family, workplace, and community.

Matthew 5:16 calls us to *"Let your good*

deeds shine out for all to see, so that everyone will praise your heavenly Father." Your faith is not just for you—it's meant to be shared.

Your Next Steps

- Reflect on each chapter's lessons and journal your thoughts.

- Set goals for your spiritual growth—daily habits that will strengthen your faith.

- Find a mentor or accountability partner to keep you on track.

- Teach what you've learned—share these principles with someone else.

You are an **Athlete of Faith.** The journey doesn't end here. Keep running, keep training, and keep living in the fullness of Christ.

A Final Prayer

From Ephesian 3:16-21:

*"I pray that from his glorious, unlimited resources he will empower you with inner strength through his Spirit. Then Christ will make his home in your hearts as you trust in him. Your roots will grow down into God's love and keep you strong. **And may you have the power to understand, as all God's people should, how wide, how long, how high, and how deep his love is.** May you experience the love of Christ, though it is too great to understand fully. Then you will be made complete with all the fullness of life and power that comes from God.*

*Now all glory to God, who is able, through his mighty power at work within us, to accomplish infinitely more than we might ask or think. Glory to him in the church and in Christ Jesus through all generations forever and ever! **Amen."***